Tom Thumb

A pantomime

Paul Reakes

Samuel French — London
www.samuelfrench-london.co.uk

© 2009 BY PAUL REAKES

Rights of Performance by Amateurs are controlled by Samuel French Ltd, 52 Fitzroy Street, London W1T 5JR, and they, or their authorized agents, issue licences to amateurs on payment of a fee. **It is an infringement of the Copyright to give any performance or public reading of the play before the fee has been paid and the licence issued.**

The Royalty Fee indicated below is subject to contract and subject to variation at the sole discretion of Samuel French Ltd.

>Basic fee for each and every
>performance by amateurs   Code K
>in the British Isles

The publication of this play does not imply that it is necessarily available for performance by amateurs or professionals, either in the British Isles or Overseas. Amateurs and professionals considering a production are strongly advised in their own interests to apply to the appropriate agents for written consent before starting rehearsals or booking a theatre or hall.

The right of Paul Reakes to be identified as author of this work has been asserted by him in accordance with Section 77 of the Copyright, Designs and Patents Act 1988

ISBN 978 0 573 16444 6

Please see page iv for further copyright information

CHARACTERS

Mum Thumb, the palace cook and cleaner
Tom Thumb } her sons
Tim Thumb }
The King
Princess Primrose, his daughter
Lucy Lastic, her maid
Slither Slugslime, the giant's henchman
The Crone
Spellena, a witch
The Giant
1st Citizen
2nd Citizen
3rd Citizen
1st Guard
2nd Guard
Chorus of Citizens, Children, Gardeners, Demons, Woodland Wildlife and **Kitchen Staff**

SYNOPSIS OF SCENES

ACT I
SCENE 1 The Royal Gardens
SCENE 2 A Country Lane
SCENE 3 Mum Thumb's cottage
SCENE 4 The Lane
SCENE 5 Throne Room of the Palace

ACT II
SCENE 1 The Weird Wood
SCENE 2 The Lane
SCENE 3 The Royal Gardens
SCENE 4 The Lane
SCENE 5 Kitchen in the Giant's Castle
SCENE 6 Before the Banquet
SCENE 7 The Grand Finale

Time - Pantotime

COPYRIGHT INFORMATION

(See also page ii)

This play is fully protected under the Copyright Laws of the British Commonwealth of Nations, the United States of America and all countries of the Berne and Universal Copyright Conventions.

All rights including Stage, Motion Picture, Radio, Television, Public Reading, and Translation into Foreign Languages, are strictly reserved.

No part of this publication may lawfully be reproduced in ANY form or by any means — photocopying, typescript, recording (including video-recording), manuscript, electronic, mechanical, or otherwise—or be transmitted or stored in a retrieval system, without prior permission.

Licences for amateur performances are issued subject to the understanding that it shall be made clear in all advertising matter that the audience will witness an amateur performance; that the names of the authors of the plays shall be included on all programmes; and that the integrity of the authors' work will be preserved.

The Royalty Fee is subject to contract and subject to variation at the sole discretion of Samuel French Ltd.

In Theatres or Halls seating Four Hundred or more the fee will be subject to negotiation.

In Territories Overseas the fee quoted above may not apply. A fee will be quoted on application to our local authorized agent, or if there is no such agent, on application to Samuel French Ltd, London.

VIDEO-RECORDING OF AMATEUR PRODUCTIONS

Please note that the copyright laws governing video-recording are extremely complex and that it should not be assumed that any play may be video-recorded for whatever purpose without first obtaining the permission of the appropriate agents. The fact that a play is published by Samuel French Ltd does not indicate that video rights are available or that Samuel French Ltd controls such rights.

MUSICAL NUMBERS

ACT I

No 1	Song and Dance	Citizens
No 2	Romantic Duet	Tom and Primrose
No 3	Comedy Song	Mum, Tim and Lucy
No 4	Dance	Demons
No 4a	Reprise of Song 4	Demons
No 5	Comedy Duet	Tim and Lucy
No 6	Song and Dance	Tom, Primrose and Citizens
No 7	Song	Mum, Tim, Lucy and Audience
No 8	Romantic Solo	Primrose

ACT II

No 9	Dance	Woodland Wildlife
No 10	Song and Dance	Tom, Mum, Tim, Lucy and Wildlife
No 10a	Reprise of Song 2	Tom
No 11	Song and Dance	Citizens
No 12	Comedy Song	The Crone
No 13	Song	Primrose, Children and Guards
No 14	Song and Dance	All
No 15	House Song	Mum, Tim, Lucy and Audience
No 16	Finale Song or Reprise	All

COPYRIGHT MUSIC

The notice printed below on behalf of the Performing Right Society should be carefully read if any copyright music is used in this play.

The permission of the owner of the performing rights in copyright music must be obtained before any public performance may be given, whether in conjunction with a play or sketch or otherwise, and this permission is just as necessary for amateur performances as for professional. The majority of copyright musical works (other than oratorios, musical plays and similar dramatico-musical works) are controlled in the British Commonwealth by the PERFORMING RIGHT SOCIETY Ltd, 29-33 Berners Street, London W1P 4AA.

The Society's practice is to issue licences authorizing the use of its repertoire to the proprietors of premises at which music is publicly performed, or, alternatively, to the organizers of musical entertainments, but the Society does not require payment of fees by performers as such. Producers or promoters of plays, sketches, etc., at which music is to be performed, during or after the play or sketch, should ascertain whether the premises at which their performances are to be given are covered by a licence issued by the Society, and if they are not, should make application to the Society for particulars as to the fee payable.

A separate and additional licence from PHONOGRAPHIC PERFORMANCES LTD, 1 Upper James Street, London W1R 3HG, is needed whenever commercial recordings are used.

CHARACTERS AND COSTUMES

Mum Thumb (Dame) is a loud and ludicrous "lady", but you can't help liking the old girl. She is always on friendly and confidential terms with the audience, and never misses an opportunity to involve them. The part also requires some skilful use of finger puppetry (see Production Notes). All her costumes, hair-dos and make-up should be outrageous and funny. Special finale costume.

Tom Thumb (Principal Boy) is the head gardener at the palace and in love with the princess. He is a handsome young man with sparkling charisma and a gorgeous pair of legs! A strong singing voice and dancing ability is required. His costume, although homespun, should be distinct in colour as it is replicated in the finger puppets (see Production Notes). Magnificent finale costume.

Tim Thumb (Comedian) is not too bright, but he is a very lovable and endearing young chap. He enjoys his own "jokes", and is involved in plenty of comic business. Ability for comedic singing and dancing is an advantage, but good camaraderie with the audience is essential, particularly with the youngsters. His costume should be comically suitable for an assistant gardener.

The King (Character part) is a very easy-going monarch. Mature in years, he is urbane, rather vague and could have stepped straight out of a P.G. Wodehouse novel. He is more concerned about his fuchsias than the imminent arrival of the giant. No singing or dancing is required. He can be arrayed in full regal finery, but a comfortable old suit of check plus-fours would fit his character better. Whatever his apparel, he always wears his crown. He also gets to wear a dented suit of armour.

Princess Primrose (Principal Girl) is a beautiful young woman who is full of natural grace and charm. She also faces up to reality, unlike her befuddled father. She loves Tom deeply despite their social differences, and stands up to the vile Slugslime when he makes his unwanted advances. A pleasant singing voice and dancing ability is called for. Needless to say all her costumes are exquisite as befitting a royal princess. Magnificent finale costume.

Lucy Lastic (Comedienne) is maid to the princess and Tim's girlfriend. She is a natural partner for Tim, being a bit dopey herself and romantically soppy when they are alone together. Like Tim she is involved in plenty of comic business and audience participation. Ability for comedic singing and dancing is an advantage, but good rapport with the audience is essential. Her costume is comically fussy and frilly.

Slither Slugslime (Baddie) is the giant's evil henchman. He is a thoroughly nasty and repulsive individual who never misses an opportunity to goad the audience into a frenzy of boos and hisses. He possesses magical powers which he uses for evil purposes, like shrinking Tom to the size of a thumb. He also fancies the princess and hopes to make her his wife. A strong dominant personality is needed for this role. No singing or dancing is required. Ideally, he should be tall and skeletal, with long, lank hair and a sinister face that is greenish in hue. His tight-fitting costume and swirling cloak should be made from a material that gives it a "slimy" unpleasant appearance.

The Crone (Comedy character part) is exactly what you would expect a witch to look like, warts and all! But she is not a witch, just someone who is unfortunate in her appearance and choice of dress. Amazingly, when her warts have been removed (by a real witch), she thinks that she looks a million dollars and goes man hunting! Ability for comedic singing is required.

Spellena (Magical character part) certainly doesn't look like a witch. But she is one! A very powerful witch who only uses her magic to bring about good. She is young and very pretty, despite the fact that she is a hundred and fifty years old! No singing or dancing required, but a clear and pleasant voice is essential. Her costume is picturesque and peasant-like in its simplicity. Special finale costume.

The Giant Before: We only see his enormous eye and hand, and hear his booming laughter and deep, menacing voice (see production notes). After: We see the whole of him, or at least the miniaturized version brought about by Spellena's magic. This is achieved by using a small child dressed as in the giant's portrait with a big bushy beard, etc.

There are several smaller speaking parts: three prominent citizens that can be either male or female, two guards (male if possible), a gardener, one of the children, and the child who plays the miniature giant.

The Chorus, Dancers and **Children** appear as Citizens, their Children, Gardeners, Demons, Woodland Wildlife and Kitchen Staff.

PRODUCTION NOTES

STAGING

The pantomime offers opportunities for elaborate staging, but can be produced quite simply if funds and facilities are limited.

There are four full sets:
    The Royal Gardens
    Mum Thumb's cottage
    Throne Room of the Palace
    Kitchen

These scenes are interlinked with tabs or one front-cloth scene:
    A Country Lane

There can be a special Finale setting, or the Royal Gardens can be used with added decorations and fairy lights.

THUMB-SIZE TOM

"Thumb-size" Tom makes his first appearance emerging from a basket on the table in Mum Thumb's cottage. (Act I, Scene 3). The following is a suggestion as to how this could be staged. You will need to obtain or construct a table that is fairly high and big enough for one person to fit comfortably underneath. The table is completely covered by a cloth that hangs to the ground. Through the cloth and the table-top a round hole is cut. You will need a fairly large basket without handles and with a hole made in its bottom. This is positioned over the hole in the table and fixed firmly in place. A person is concealed under the table and operates a "thumb-size" Tom finger puppet from below. The puppeteer should be in position at the beginning of the scene. To try and take up the position during the black-out is not recommended. The "thumb-size" Tom finger puppet must be large enough to be seen from the back of the auditorium. A spotlight will help. To add to the illusion, the puppet should be clothed in a distinctive colour that matches the costume worn by the full size Tom Thumb.
We next see "thumb-size" Tom being transported in the basket by Mum Thumb (Act I, Scene 4) You will need a duplicate of the basket used in the previous scene with its bottom removed. Mum Thumb, assuming "she" is right-handed, cradles the basket in the crook of her left arm and operates the "thumb-size" Tom finger puppet with her right hand. I would strongly advise that Mum has use of the puppet and basket early in rehearsals. Plenty of practice at manipulation and her one-sided conversation with tiny Tom will help to create the illusion that he is really there. The same puppet can be used, but I suggest you have a

couple on stand-by. (You don't want the poor little chap getting lost!) When the lights come up after the black-out in Act II, Scene 1, the basket is seen lying on the ground. Tim must quickly retrieve it and conceal its open bottom. He will also require a complete basket to bring on in Act II, Scene 3. This means you will need three identical baskets in all.

THE GIANT

In this pantomime I have chosen to show only parts of the giant. These consist of one enormous eye and one huge hand. Both make their appearance in the Throne Room scene (Act I, Scene 5).
The Eye: It is seen through a window in the back wall of the set. This window should be a simple arched opening. The eye can be painted on a flat panel that slides into view between the window and the backcloth or cyclorama. This is a simple method, and a more elaborate effect is encouraged. For instance, an animated eyeball and eyelid would be terrific! The ingenuity of set designers and backstage crews holds no bounds!
The Hand: I have not specified from which side of the stage this monstrous appendage appears. Wing space can be cramped, but there is usually more room on one side than the other. The hand can be a simple painted cut out that slides on to the stage. But, as with the eye, a more elaborate effect might be attempted. Huge fingers that actually move would be fantastic! Also, the acting skill of Princess Primrose as she appears to be struggling in the giant's grasp will help.

LIGHTING AND EFFECTS

All the usual elements are required for a tale of magic and fantasy. These include: blinding flashes, black-outs, thunder claps, lightning flashes, giant footsteps, magical sounds, dramatic and romantic lighting changes. There is an exploding tea urn in Act I, and a bag and bunch of flowers that appear to move by themselves (with help of nylon lines) in Act II. An off stage microphone is required to give us the giant's booming laughter and menacing voice. There are opportunities for imaginative and atmospheric lighting. Very spooky and sinister to accompany Slugslime's evil doings, and magical enchantment for when Spellena, the good witch, displays her powers. Extra use of follow spots for songs, individual characters and audience participation business is left to the director.

The time is Pantotime. This means that the style of settings and costumes can be a fantastical mixture of all periods.

Paul Reakes

Other works by Paul Reakes
published by Samuel French Ltd

Pantomimes

Babes in the Wood
Bluebeard
Cinderella
Dick Turpin
Goody Two Shoes
King Arthur
King Humpty Dumpty
Little Jack Horner
Little Miss Muffet
Little Red Riding Hood
Little Tommy Tucker
Old Mother Hubbard
Robinson Crusoe and the Pirates
Santa in Space
Sinbad the Sailor

Plays

Bang, You're Dead!
Mantrap

ACT I

Scene 1

The Royal Gardens

Full set. UR, *steps lead to a side entrance of the Royal Palace. The backcloth and groundrow show the rest of the palace with its abundant and beautiful gardens. Side wings represent trees, bushes and flower beds*

When the CURTAIN *rises, the 2nd and 3rd Citizens are discovered. They go straight into the opening song and dance*

Song 1

After the number, the 1st Citizen enters from L, *looking morose*

1st Citizen Huh! I don't know what you lot have got to sing and dance about.
2nd Citizen We're waiting for the king to give us our free fruit and veg from the royal gardens.
1st Citizen Well, you'd better make the most of it. Pretty soon there won't be any more fruit and veg. Or any other kind of food for that matter.
3rd Citizen What are you talking about?
1st Citizen The giant! That's what I'm talking about!
2nd Citizen But he's hundreds of miles away in the kingdom of Pantomania.
1st Citizen Ah, but for how long? The people of Pantomania have had to give him all their food. If they refuse he takes their women and children hostage. They're all starving to death! Now, what do you suppose will happen when the food there runs out? The giant will come *here*, that's what he'll do!

2nd and 3rd Citizens react with horror

Not singing and dancing now, are we?

3rd Citizen This is serious. I hope the king's going to do something about it.
1st Citizen Huh! He's probably too busy fussing over his fuschias or cuddling his cucumbers.

Princess Primrose and her maid, Lucy Lastic, enter from the palace

Primrose Good-morning, everyone.
Citizens (*without enthusiasm*) Good-morning, Your Highness.

Primrose and Lucy come down the steps

Primrose Oh, dear! You all look rather glum. Is something the matter?
2nd Citizen Your Highness, we've just been hearing about the giant in Pantomania.
3rd Citizen He's eating all the food there and everyone is starving!
2nd Citizen And he's taking women and children hostage!
3rd Citizen Are these stories true, Your Highness?
Primrose (*sadly*) Yes. I'm afraid they are.
1st Citizen (*smugly*) Told ya so!
2nd Citizen What will happen if the giant decides to come here and do the same to us?
Citizens Yes!
Primrose Believe me, I share your concern. (*Trying her best to sound reassuring*) The king is well aware of the situation. It goes without saying that his main concern is for the safety of our kingdom.
1st Citizen But what's he gonna do about it? That's what we want to know.
Citizens Yes!
Primrose I intend to raise the subject with him again this morning.
1st Citizen (*looking towards the palace entrance*) Well, now's your chance! Here he comes!

A fanfare is sounded

The King enters from the palace

King (*very bright and breezy*) Good-morning, good-morning, good-morning! Is everybody happy? (*He is oblivious to the troubled atmosphere as he comes down the steps*) Capital! Capital! That's what I like to hear.
Primrose Father, I must speak with you.
King Certainly, m'dear, certainly. As the rabbit said — I'm all ears! (*He gives a jovial laugh*) Ha! Ha!

Act I, Scene 1

Primrose The people are very concerned.
King Are they?
Citizens Yes!
King (*to the Citizens*) Well, you needn't be. There's plenty of fruit and veg to go round. You'll all get your fair share as usual. Young Tom Thumb, my head gardener, is at this very moment supervising the final picking, plucking and pulling. Soon you'll be able to take away as much fresh fruit and vegetables as you can carry. There! What d'you say to that?

The Citizens go into a huddle L

I say! What's up with 'em, Primrose? They don't seem very enthusiastic, do they?
Primrose (*taking him* R) Father. You must listen to me.
King What is it, m'dear?

Tom Thumb enters at the back. He is followed by his brother Tim and a couple of Gardeners

Tom Morning all!
King Ah! Here he is! Tom Thumb, my head gardener!
Tom (*coming down and giving a stately bow*) Good-morning, Your Majesty. (*Bows to Primrose*) Good-morning, Your Highness.
Primrose Good-morning, Tom.
Tim (*doing his idea of a stately bow*) Good-morning, Your Regalships!
Primrose }
King } (*together*) Good-morning, Tim.
Tim (*moving to Lucy, all soppy*) Mornin', Lucy.
Lucy (*equally soppy*) Mornin', Timmy.

Comic business as they playfully nudge each other and giggle

King Well, is everything ready, Tom?
Tom Yes, Your Majesty. It's all picked and waiting for collection. (*To the Citizens*) There's enough fresh fruit and vegetables to keep you going for weeks.
Tim Especially the rhubarb! (*He guffaws*)
Tom (*to the unresponsive Citizens*) Well, aren't you going to thank His Majesty for giving you this free produce?
Tim Yes. Just think how much it would cost at (*local shop*)!
King No thanks are required. We grow far more than we need at the palace. It would only go to waste.

Tom Show them where it is, Tim.
Tim Right-oh! This way, folks!

Tim and Lucy usher the Citizens out at the back and exit with them. The King follows them out

Primrose Tom, I need your help.
Tom You only have to ask.
Primrose It's about the giant in Pantomania. Our people are worried that he's going to come here.
Tom I think their worries are justified.
Primrose So do I. I've tried talking to my father about it, but he just pretends it's not going to happen. Help me talk to him, Tom. Help me make him see the seriousness of the situation.
Tom Of course I will. (*After a quick look to make sure they are alone, he takes her hands. Tenderly*) I'd do anything for you, Primrose, you know that. (*They embrace*) When are we going to tell your father about us?
Primrose That's an even bigger problem than the giant. I can't imagine what his reaction will be when he finds out that his only daughter and his head gardener are in love with each other.
Tom I don't care what he thinks. I don't care what *anyone* thinks. I love you, Primrose. And I'll never stop loving you.

Song 2

A romantic duet with romantic lighting. After the number, the lighting returns to normal

The King enters at the back

Tom and Primrose part quickly

The King comes down to them, rubbing his hands and laughing

King Ha! Ha! You should see 'em! Pouncing on that fruit and veg like Tesco before a bank holiday!
Primrose Father, Tom and I need to talk to you.
King Certainly, m'dear. (*He takes a gardening magazine from his pocket*) Had this come this morning, Tom. Jolly interesting. (*Opens it and reads*)
Primrose Father, please. This is serious.
King I should say it is! (*Showing Tom something in the magazine*) Look at the size of that chap's hollyhocks!

Act I, Scene 1

Tom Your Majesty, we need to talk about something that concerns the safety of the kingdom.

King What? It's not those perishin' snails again, is it? Tried throwin' 'em over the fence, but they just came marchin' back again! Perhaps we should write to (*TV gardener*) about it.

Tom It's got nothing to do with the garden, Your Majesty. It's about the giant in Pantomania.

King (*dismissively*) Oh, that! (*Looking in the magazine*) I say! Aren't they lovely! D'you think we should get some for the south-facing border?

Primrose (*snatching the book away from him*) Father! Listen to me! The giant is terrorising the people there! He's taking all their food. Everyone is starving.

Tom And if they refuse he's taking women and children hostage. Sire, your people are worried that the same thing is going to happen here.

King Nonsense! They're worrying unduly. The giant won't come here.

Primrose How can you be so sure?

King My dear, Pantomania is hundreds of miles away. He's not going to come all that distance.

Tom A few hundred miles is nothing to a giant. A couple of big strides and he's here!

Primrose Tom is right. (*Desperately*) Oh, Father, you must realize the terrible threat we're under.

King (*putting a soothing arm around her*) Now, now, my dear. Don't get yourself in a state. That naughty old giant isn't going to bother us. (*Taking the magazine*) Don't you worry your pretty head about it. (*He goes up the steps, looking at the magazine*) Yes! I'm definitely going to get some of these. Oh! And some of those!

He exits into the palace

Tom Well, we tried our best. Perhaps he's right. Perhaps the giant won't come here after all.

Primrose Do you honestly believe that?

Tom No, not really.

Primrose How long do you think it will be before he comes here?

Tom Well, the food in Pantomania is bound to run out pretty soon, and then ... (*He shrugs*) At least we'll get a warning if he's heading our way.

Primrose A warning?

Tom Yes. If he's hungry we'll be able to hear his enormous stomach rumbling.

Primrose (*smiling in spite of herself*) Oh, Tom!

Tom (*moving close to her*) That's better. I hate to see you looking so unhappy. (*Taking her hand*) Come on. Let's try talking to your father again.

Tom and Primrose exit DR

Tim and Lucy enter at the back

Tim I bet you've never seen one as big as mine, Lucy.
Lucy No. It's ginormous!
Tim I don't show it to just anyone. (*Getting all soppy*) But you're special, Lucy.
Lucy Am I, Timmy? (*She cuddles up to him*) It was nice of you to show it to me, Timmy.
Tim It's a beauty, innit? The biggest vegetable marrow this side of (*local place*)!
Lucy You must be ever so clever to grow something that big. You must have green fingers.
Tim I have! Except when I'm putting manure on the rose beds. (*He guffaws*)
Lucy What do you *do* with a marrow?
Tim Stuff it!
Lucy (*pouting*) I was only asking!
Tim No, that's what you do with it! You stuff it, cook it an' eat it.
Lucy (*cuddling up to him*) Oh, Timmy! You know about so many things.
Tim I know! I'm a right clever clogs, I am!

Tim and Lucy canoodle

One of the Gardeners appears from L

Gardener Hey, Tim! Where's your mum with the tea?
Tim I dunno.
Gardener Well, find her! We're all dying of thirst out here!

He exits L

Tim I suppose we'd better give her a shout. (*Calling*) Mum!
Lucy (*calling*) Mum Thumb!
Tim Mum!
Lucy Mum Thumb!
Tim Mum!

Act I, Scene 1

Mum (*off* DR, *calling*) All right! All right! Keep yer hair on! I'm comin' as fast as I can!

Mum Thumb enters from DR, *pushing a trolley. It contains a "Heath Robinson" style tea urn, cups and boxes of biscuits, etc.*

Mum (*pushing the trolley to* C) I'm 'ere! I'm 'ere! What's all the fuss about? It's not the (*local reference*) in trouble again, is it?
Tim Hallo, Mum!
Mum Hallo, Timmy! (*Observing Lucy*) Oh! I see you've got (*current model/celebrity*) with you.
Lucy Hallo, Mum Thumb. Timmy's just been showing me his great big marrow.
Mum (*with suspicion*) I see. I hope that's all he's been showing you.
Tim You're late, Mum.
Mum I know I am! There's no need to state the oblivious! I'm late because — (*with a dramatic sigh*) I've had a bit of trouble.
Lucy Oh, dear.
Tim Have you been to the doctor?
Mum What can *he* do? I've been to the (*local*) garage!

Tim and Lucy react to this

But they say it's a hopeless case. (*Dramatically*) We've got to face the awful truth. I need a new tea urn! (*Patting the tea urn*) Poor old Ernestine's on her last legs.

Lucy and Tim burst out laughing

Mum What's so funny?
Lucy A new tea urn!
Tim We thought you were talking about yourself!
Mum You thought ... (*to the audience, absently*) What a pair of wallies! (*She does a huge "double take" at the audience, and then lets out a yell*) YAAAGH!!! (*She staggers back against the trolley*)
Tim What's the matter, Mum?
Mum You ... you didn't tell me we had company!
Lucy What company?
Mum (*pointing to the audience*) Them company!

Tim and Lucy come forward and peer out at the audience

Tim Well, dangle my dibber! Where did they come from?

Lucy Have they been here all the time?

They continue to gape open-mouthed at the audience. Mum recovers and pushes in between Lucy and Tim

Mum Don't just stand there with your mouths open like a couple of goldfish! Be polite. (*To audience*) Hallo.

A few replies

>(*To Tim*) I think they've dozed off! (*To audience*) I said (*bellowing*) HALLO!

The audience shout back, and all three react

>That's better. I am Mrs Thumb. Commonly known as Mum Thumb. I'm the cook and general fat totem at the royal palace. (*Indicating Tim*) This poor excuse for a garden gnome is my son Timmy. (*To him*) Well, go on! Say something!

Tim Something! (*He guffaws*)
Mum That's what you get for sendin' 'em to (*local school/college*) Have you seen Tom, my other son? Oh, he's a lovely lad, isn't he? He's the head gardener here, and —

Lucy nudges Mum, eager to be introduced

>(*To Lucy*) What is it? Oh, yes. This is Lucy Lastic.

Lucy (*to audience*) I'm maid to Princess Primrose. (*She performs an awkward curtsy*)
Mum Made to fall apart by the look of it! She and Timmy have an understanding. Mind you, nobody else does!
Tim (*with his hand up*) Mum! Mum!
Mum You know where it is.
Tim No, I've just had a thought.
Mum Well, look after it because it's on strange ground.
Tim Perhaps they'd like some tea and biscuits.
Mum That's a very thoughtful thunk, my little water feature. (*To audience*) Would you like some tea? (*To someone*) Yes, I know what you'd like, dear! So would I, but I haven't got a licence. It's tea or nothin'. (*She takes boxes of biscuits from the trolley, and gives them to Tim and Lucy*) Right! You two go and hand out the bikkies and take orders for tea.

Act I, Scene 1 9

Tim and Lucy look nervously at the audience

Well, go on! They won't bite. By the look of it most of 'em have left their teeth at home.

The house lights come up

Tim and Lucy go down into the auditorium. Ad-lib and comic by-play as they go amongst the audience handing out small packets of biscuits.
Mum busies herself at the trolley. NOTE: If the exploding tea urn sequence requires that the trolley should be near a side wing, Mum can position it there at this point

Tim Mum?
Mum (*coming forward*) Yes, Timmy. Have you got an order?
Tim This lady wants to know if the tea is China or Indian?
Mum Neither! It's from (*local store*)! (*She busies herself at the urn*)

Tim and Lucy continue to move about among the audience

Lucy Mum Thumb?
Mum (*coming forward*) Yes?
Lucy This gentleman wants to know if you can give him a good Darjeeling.
Mum Ooo! The cheeky monkey! Who does he think I am! I ... (*on second thoughts*) What's he look like? How old is he?
Lucy It's hard to tell.
Mum Is he breathing?
Lucy A bit.
Mum That's good enough! Tell him I knock off at five and I'll meet him round the back of (*local place*). And tell him to bring his own Sanatogen.

She goes back to the urn as Tim and Lucy move about among the audience

Tim Mum?
Mum (*coming forward*) 'Allo!
Tim This lady wants to know if you've got Lapsang?
Mum No, it's just the way this dress hangs. (*Business with costume*) I got it off the peg in (*local shop*).
Tim Looks like they left the peg in!
Mum Watch it, you! Stop messin' about and come back 'ere!

Tim and Lucy return to the stage

The house lights go down

Mum (*looking in the boxes*) Typical! All the Kit Kats (*or whatever*) are gone! You might as well have the rest!

They throw the remaining packets of biscuits to the audience

Tim Is the tea ready, Mum?
Mum Nearly. It's brewing. You'd better find something to do while we're waitin'.

Tim and Lucy start cuddling

Not that! *Not that!* (*She pulls them apart. To Tim*) I'll stop you watching that (*TV Nature programme*)! Let's have a song.

Song 3

Song for Mum, Tim and Lucy

Mum (*going to trolley*) Right! (*Stroking the tea urn, lovingly*) Now, don't you let me down Ernestine. One delicious cuppa comin' up.

She places a cup under the urn's spout and turns the tap. Nothing happens. She turns it again and still nothing

Lucy Nothing's coming out.
Mum I know (*mimicking Lucy*) "nothing's coming out"! Oh! (*Frustrated, she tries the taps again. Nothing*)
Tim Shall I call "Dyno-rod"?
Mum There's no need. (*Stroking the urn*) She's a bit delicate, that's all. She's like me.
Tim Clapped out, y'mean. (*He guffaws*)
Mum Watch it, you! All she needs is a little TLC.
Tim Don't you mean TNT? (*He guffaws*)

Mum takes up a large mallet. Tim reacts and hides behind Lucy

Mum gives the urn a hefty whack with the mallet. The urn starts to vibrate and make strange, gurgling noises

Act I, Scene 1

Mum, Tim and Lucy back away nervously to the other side of the stage

The urn's vibrations and noises increase. Mum, Tim and Lucy huddle together in terror

Lucy Oh, Timmy! What's it doing?!

The urn starts rocking about and the noise has changed to a loud, high-pitched whine

Tim (*to audience*) Don't just sit there! *Take cover!*
Mum *She's gonna BLOW!!!*

They cower away and cover their ears

There is a blinding flash and a loud bang as the urn explodes. If possible, the lid of the urn flies off. Smoke billows out

Very cautiously, Mum and the others creep across to inspect the damage

(*To audience*) Sorry, folks. Tea's off!

Tom and Primrose rush on from DR

The Citizens and Gardeners rush on at the back

Tom What's happening? Mum! Are you all right?
Mum Yes, Tom. But poor old Ernestine's finally blown her top.

The King enters from the palace and comes down to join the others

King I say! What on earth's going on out here? What was that dreadful noise?
Mum It was Ernestine.
King Oh, dear! The poor woman! Was it something she ate?
Mum She exploded!
King Good heavens! Didn't we ought to get a doctor? Or (*looking about*) organize a search party?
Tom Mum's talking about her tea urn, Your Majesty. She calls it Ernestine.
King Oh, I see! (*Doubtfully*) Do I?
Mum (*pointing to the trolley*) There she is! (*Tragically*) What's left of her!

King Oh, I say! I'm most terribly sorry. Have you known her long?
Mum Ever since she was a thermos flask! (*To Tim*) You'd better take her away and give her a decent burial.

Tim and Lucy push the trolley off stage and return immediately

Mum May she — *rust in pieces*! I'm sorry about the noise, Your Royal Jelly.
King Don't mention it. I just wondered what all the fuss was about.
1st Citizen (*as morose as ever*) So did we! We thought it was the giant!
Citizens Yes!
King (*addressing the crowd in quite a kingly manner for him*) Now listen to me all of you! Let's get this nonsense sorted out once and for all. Your worries are completely unfounded. I assure you that you have nothing to fear. The giant will not be coming here. I repeat — he will not be coming here!

There is a blinding flash of lightning and a loud clap of thunder. The stage becomes dark and sinister. All react

Mum Oh, no! Not another power cut! (*or some local/topical remark to suit*)

Suddenly, several little Demons spring on from DR, *brandishing tridents*

Mum, King, Tom, Primrose, Tim, Lucy, Citizens and Gardeners back away from them to L. *More Demons spring on from* DL. *Using their tridents, the Demons force the group upstage where they form a terrified huddle*

The Demons go into their wild and weird dance

Song 4

Demon Dance with special lighting. It ends in a grotesque tableau. After the applause, the Demons face L, *kneel and bow their heads*

There is a flash and a puff of smoke

The repulsive and sinister figure of Slither Slugslime appears from DL

The lighting becomes brighter, but still remains eerie and sinister

Act I, Scene 1

Slugslime (*laughing demoniacally*) Ha! Ha! Ha!
Mum Crikey! It's (*current personality to suit*)!

At a gesture from Slugslime, the Demons retreat to DR, *where they crouch in readiness*

Mum, King, Tom, Primrose, Tim, Lucy, Citizens and Gardeners edge nervously forward from the back

King (*to Slugslime*) What is the meaning of this? Who are you?
Slugslime I am Slugslime!
Mum We can see that! But what's your name?
Slugslime That *is* my name, you ignorant old hag!
Mum (*affronted*) Oy! Not so much of the old! (*To audience*) I don't think I'm gonna like him very much!
Slugslime My full name is Slither Slippery Slinky Slugslime.
Tim I don't think his parents liked him very much either.
King What is your business here?
Slugslime My business is my master's business.
Tom Who *is* your master?
Slugslime Can't you guess? He is a mighty monumental mountain of magnificent malevolence!
Mum (*to audience*) Try sayin' that after you've had a few! (*To Slugslime*) Cut the commercials, Mr Slimy! Who is he?
Slugslime *THE GIANT!*

There is flash of lightning and a clap of thunder. Slugslime gives his evil laugh. The Demons cackle fiendishly and wave their tridents. Horrified reactions from the others

I see you have heard of him.
All Oh, yes, we've heard of him!
Primrose He's been terrorizing the poor people of Pantomania. He's reduced them to starvation, and taken women and children hostage.
Slugslime (*moving to Primrose*) A very charming appraisal of my master's achievements. (*Leering at her*) And you're very charming as well. *Very* charming indeed.
Tom (*stepping between them*) This is Her Royal Highness, the Princess Primrose. I'll ask you to show some respect.
Slugslime And who are you?
Tom (*proudly*) Tom Thumb. Head gardener.
Slugslime (*sneering*) A common dirt scratcher!
Mum And I'm his mother! Head cook and cleaner!

Slugslime A common scrubber!
Tim And *I'm* his brother!
Slugslime And what are you the head of?
Tim (*stumped*) Er ... the stairs?
King (*very regal*) And I am the king! (*He points to his crown*)
Slugslime Really? I thought you were going to a fancy dress party! (*He gives his evil laugh*)

The Demons cackle

King This is outrageous! State your business and be gone from here.
Slugslime (*with a mocking bow*) As you wish. The food supply in Pantomania has finally dried up. My master finds it necessary to look elsewhere to satisfy his gargantuan appetite. He has decided to honour this miserable kingdom with his august presence.

Groans and lamentations from the others

Mum Y'mean the giant's coming *here*?!
Slugslime (*sneering*) My, how quick you are.
Tom *When* is he coming?
Slugslime When? He is already here! He and his castle arrived a short time ago.
King His castle! How can that be? It would take years to build a castle big enough for a giant!
Slugslime (*sneering*) In the ordinary way, yes. But with my *magical* powers anything is possible.
Mum Oh, I've heard it all now! He's not only the giant's dogsbody, he thinks he's Harry Potter as well.
Tim What a load of rubbish! Magical powers indeed! If he's a magician, I'm (*current beauty*)!!

Mum and Tim laugh together

Slugslime (*sneering*) Very well, you disbelieving dolts! I see a demonstration is called for! (*He raises his arms*)
　　　　　By the powers of darkness invested in me,
　　　　　I will give you a sample of my sorcery!
　　　　　I summon the forces of warlocks and witches!
　　　　　May you both be plagued by a thousand itches!
(*Makes magic pass at Mum and Tim*) *ATMAZOOOM!!*

Act I, Scene 1

Mum and Tim are struck by the spell. They go into an uncontrollable frenzy of scratching themselves and each other. Slugslime and the Demons find it highly amusing. The others are awestruck

Mum
Tim } (*together*) Ooo! Stop! Make it stop! Aaagh! Stop it! Stop it!!

Slugslime waves his hand and the spell is broken. Mum and Tim cling to each other, exhausted and gasping for breath

Mum (*to audience*) Oooo! That's taken it right out of me, girls!
Slugslime (*to others*) Does that convince you of my powers?
All (*weakly*) Yes.
Slugslime It was only a very mild example. I am capable of much, *much* worse! Ha! Ha! Ha! (*He gives his evil laugh*)

The Demons cackle in response

Enough of these pleasantries! Here are your orders. Each day you will deliver all items of food to the giant's castle.
All *All the food?*
Slugslime Every single scrap!
Tom And what are we supposed to live on?
Slugslime (*sneering*) Try fresh air.
Mum There's not much of that since you arrived! Phew!
King And what if we refuse these demands?
All Yes!
Slugslime For each day that you refuse to comply with the giant's wishes, he will take one woman and one child hostage.
Lucy What does he do to them?
Slugslime Well, let's put it like this. (*With evil relish*) If he doesn't get his food one way, he will get it another.
Lucy You mean he ... he ... (*she gestures towards her mouth*)?
Slugslime Exactly. (*He does an impression of Hannibal Lecter*) With some baked beans and a nice Chianti.
Lucy (*wailing and clinging to Tim*) Waaaaa!!!
Slugslime So, unless you wish to end up as the dish of the day, I would strongly advise you to obey my master's instructions.

All are downcast and despondent

Come! Cheer up. Just think how slim you'll be! (*To Mum*) Particularly *you*! Ha! Ha! Ha!

Slugslime sweeps out DL, *laughing his evil laugh*

The Demons perform a short reprise of their dance, accompanied by special lighting

Song 4b (Reprise)

The reprise ends with a tableau, and the Lights fade to Black-out

Music to cover the scene change, and then the Lights come up on —

Scene 2

A country lane

Tabs, or a front cloth showing pleasant countryside dominated by the giant's forbidding castle in the distance. Entrances DR *and* DL

Slugslime enters DR *and moves to* C

Slugslime (*snarling to off* R) Come on! Hurry up, you lazy lot of layabouts!

> *Four citizens file on from* DR. *The first carries a large basket of bread. The second, a huge truckle of cheese. The third, a pile of cans. The fourth, a tall cake. They stagger across and out* DL
>
> (*as they pass in front of him*) Get a move on! Take that food to the giant's castle at once! He's feeling peckish again! Hurry up! (*Snarling to off* R) Keep it moving! Keep it moving!
>
> *One of the children enters* DR, *holding the end of a long string of large sausages. He has gone out* DL *before a second child enters* DR, *holding the other end*
>
> *Second child goes out* DL

Slugslime turns to the audience with his evil laugh

> Ha! Ha! Ha! Silence! I said — *silence!* (*To someone*) That applies to you, as well! So far the miserable minions of this kingdom have obeyed the giant's orders. Each day they bring all their food to his castle. (*Indicates castle on front cloth*) But I have my suspicions that

Act I, Scene 2

there are some who are keeping food back for themselves. (*With an evil chuckle*) But fear not. I will soon find out who they are, and when I do, they will wish they had never been born! Ha! Ha! Ha! And if I discover that you have been helping them, you will also suffer a dreadful fate! Ha! Ha! Ha!

Laughing his evil laugh, he sweeps out DL

Tim and Lucy enter from DR. *They are looking very miserable*

Tim (*greeting the audience*) Hallo, folks! (*Groaning and holding his stomach*) Ooo! I'm starving!
Lucy So am I!
Tim I'm so hungry I could eat a dinner at (*local school/café*)! All I've had today are three fingernails! Thank goodness I didn't cut my toenails!
Lucy Why?
Tim They're for lunch tomorrow! (*Shaking his fist at the castle*) That rotten, greedy old giant!
Lucy Why does he have to eat *all* our food? Surely there must be something he doesn't like. I hope he gets sick!
Tim I don't! Just imagine the mess if a giant's sick! Ugh! (*He groans and holds his stomach*) Oooo! My stomach thinks my throat's cut!
Lucy (*cuddling up to him*) Never mind, Timmy. We've still got each other.
Tim Yes, Lucy. I can always nibble your ear and pretend it's a nice big juicy steak. (*He does so*)
Lucy (*squirming*) Oooo! That tickles!
Tim (*weakly*) Oh, it's no use! I haven't even got the strength for a nibble. What's gonna happen to us, Lucy?
Lucy We'll just have to live off the fruits of love.
Tim The fruits of love?
Lucy Yes. Come here! (*Hugging him very tightly*)
Tim (*wincing*) Oooh! I think you've just squashed a pear!

Song 5

A comedy duet and dance. After the number, Lucy and Tim cling weakly to each other, holding their stomachs and groaning

Mum Thumb's head appears DR. *She is acting very secretively*

Mum Psst! Psst! (*Crouching low, she creeps over to them*)
Tim What's the matter, Mum? Had an accident?

Mum I've got something.
Tim (*backing away*) Ugh! Is it catching?!
Mum I've got — you know what! (*She taps her nose*)
Lucy A cold?
Mum No! You know what. (*She gives a big wink*)
Tim Something in your eye?
Mum (*losing patience*) No, you pair of plonkers! (*Back to being secretive*) I've got F.O.O.D.
Tim (*dumbly*) F.O.O.D? (*To audience*) What does that spell, kids?
Audience *Food*!
Mum (*to audience*) Shhh! Shhh! Not so loud. We don't want old Slugslime finding out.
Tim (*excited*) Food! Well done, Mum! Where is it?
Mum I have it secreted about my person!

Tim and Lucy react and look at her

 (*To the audience*) I know I'm gonna regret asking this! (*To Mum*) Where?

Mum makes a big thing of looking about. Tim and Lucy do the same and all three get into a hopeless tangle. Eventually they sort themselves out. Mum reaches down the front of her dress. Comic contortions as she fishes about trying to find something

 (*To the audience*) It's alive whatever it is!

Finally Mum extracts a large wedge of cheese

Tim
Lucy } (*together, ecstatically*) *Cheese!!*
Mum Much longer down there and it would have been toasted!
Tim
Lucy } (*together, reaching out*) Give us some! Give us some!
Mum (*fending them off*) Ger off! We've got to make sure the coast is clear first. We don't want Mr Slimy creepin' up on us, do we?
Tim Our mates out there'll keep watch for us. Won't you, folks?
Audience Yes!
Lucy (*to audience*) You'll give us a shout if you see him, won't you?
Audience Yes!
Mum And if you're really good I might give you a bit. (*Reaction*) *Of cheese*! Ooo! The minds of some people! (*To Tim and Lucy*) Come on! Let's get our choppers into the cheddar!

Act I, Scene 2   19

They move to C *and prepare to eat the cheese*

   Slugslime enters from DL *and creeps up behind them*
The audience starts shouting warnings

Mum (*to audience*) What's up? Is it Mr Slimy?
Audience Yes!
Lucy Are you sure?
Audience Yes!
Tim Where is he?
Audience He's behind you!
Mum (*to Tim and Lucy*) We'd better have a look.

Comic business as they turn slowly around with Slugslime keeping behind them

Mum (*facing the back*) He's not here!
Tim Where is he now?
Audience Behind you!

They turn slowly to face front with Slugslime still behind them

Mum No, he's not! (*To Tim*) I think they're havin' us on.
Tim Yeah! (*To audience*) Stop messin' about. (*To Mum*) Come on! Let's have some of that cheese!

He grabs the cheese from Mum. Tim, Lucy and Mum should be in a straight line with Tim L, *Lucy* C *and Mum* R

Tim goes to take a bite of cheese and Slugslime moves to his L. *Mum sees him and nudges Lucy, who in turn nudges Tim. Tim sees Slugslime and quickly passes the cheese to Lucy, who quickly passes it on to Mum. Mum has no one to pass it to, so she just drops it on the ground*

All three face front, trying to appear unconcerned. Slugslime walks slowly behind them to the right of Mum. He picks up the cheese

Slugslime What is this?
Mum Er ... is it a doorstop?
Slugslime It looks remarkably like a piece of cheese to me.
Mum Oh, yes! So it does. I thought there was a funny smell. I put it down to you.
Slugslime What is it doing here?

Mum I ... er ... I think a mouse dropped it.
Slugslime (*sneering*) Yes! (*Giving Mum the once-over*) A very *large* mouse with peculiar-looking hair and terrible dress sense!
Mum (*to Lucy*) Ooo! 'Ark at Trinny and Susannah!
Slugslime Ah! Then you admit it's yours!
Mum I admit nothing. I wish to plead unsanitary!
Slugslime So! You have been keeping back food for yourselves, have you? (*He walks behind them to* L) I had my suspicions that this sort of thing was going on. You have deliberately disobeyed orders and for that you must be made an example of!

Tim, Mum and Lucy quake with fear and cling to each other

I will take you to the giant! (*With relish*) You three will provide a very tasty snack for him! (*Laughing his evil laugh, he moves away to* DL) Ha! Ha! Ha!
Lucy Ooo! He's gonna feed us to the giant!
Tim What are we gonna do, Mum?
Mum I have a cunning plan! (*To audience*) We'll need your help, folks! Play along with us! (*Moving to Slugslime*) Excuse me, Mr Slug Pellet. Sorry to interrupt you in mid cackle, but there's something you should know.
Slugslime What?
Mum We're not the only ones hiding food. (*Pointing to the audience*) They've got some as well!
Slugslime (*scrutinizing the audience*) Have they?
Mum Oh, yes! Stacks of it! (*To audience, shaking her head and indicating for them to say no*) Haven't you?
Audience No!
Slugslime (*to audience*) Oh, yes, you have!
Audience Oh, no, we haven't!

As the exchange continues between Slugslime and the audience, Mum creeps away and pushes Tim and Lucy off stage DR

She then gives the audience the "thumbs up" and dashes out after them

Eventually, Slugslime discovers they have gone

Slugslime (*roaring with anger*) Curses! They've got away! COME BACK!!!

Waving the cheese, Slugslime runs out DR

Act I, Scene 3   21

The Lights fade to Black-out

Music is played to cover the scene change

Scene 3

Mum Thumb's cottage

Full set. The backcloth and side wings represent the interior of a picturesque cottage. Back C is a fairly high practical table with a cloth that reaches to the ground. On the table, among other items, is a basket. (See Production Notes.) Entrances R and L

The Lights come up on Tom, Princess Primrose and the Citizens. They are engaged in a song and dance

Song 6

Tom That was great. I'm glad to see you're all looking a lot happier than when you arrived.
2ⁿᵈ Citizen We are, Tom, thanks to you.
Citizens Ay!
3ʳᵈ Citizen We can't thank you enough for giving us something to eat.
Citizens Ay!
Tom It was only some bread and jam. I wish I had more to give you.
Primrose You must be careful, Tom. If Slugslime found out that you were secretly supplying food to people there's no knowing what he might do.
2ⁿᵈ Citizen The princess is right. You don't want to get into trouble with him on our account.
1ˢᵗ Citizen (*as grumpy as ever*) There wouldn't be any trouble if the king had done something to prevent the giant coming here in the first place!
Tom And what could he have done? Told the giant all our food was past its sell-by date?

The others laugh, which deflates the 1ˢᵗ Citizen

Tom We've just got to grin and bear it, I'm afraid. And what Slugslime doesn't know about won't hurt him.

Mum, Tim and Lucy dash on from R. They bend over, gasping for air

Primrose Mum Thumb! Tim! Lucy! What's wrong?

Tom What's happened, Mum?
Mum (*clinging to him and gasping*) Ooo! ... Tom! ... There's a man after me!
Tom That's never worried you before.
Mum I know, but this one's different! It's that 'orrible slimy Slugslime!
Tom What have you been up to?
Tim He found out Mum had some secret cheese!
Lucy We were just about to eat it when he caught us!
Mum We managed to slip through his grasp, but he's comin' after us!
Slugslime (*off* R, *yelling*) Where are you?!
Lucy Oooh! That's him now!
Mum You haven't seen us, right?

Mum dashes out L, *followed by Tim and Lucy*

A second later, Slugslime enters from R

Slugslime (*looking about*) Where are they? (*Snarling at Tom*) Where are you hiding them?
Tom (*casually*) Who are you looking for?
Slugslime Your mother, your numbskull brother and that soppy girlfriend of his!
Tom Oh, them. They're not here at the moment. As you can see. What have they done?
Slugslime They have disobeyed orders! Withholding food that belongs to the giant! And if I find out that you are harbouring them you will be made to suffer! (*To Citizens*) All of you! (*He notices one of the children*) You!
Child Me?
Slugslime Yes, you! Come here!

The child comes forward with obvious tell-tale signs of jam around the mouth

Slugslime What is that on your face?
Child Skin!
Slugslime It looks suspiciously like strawberry jam to me!

He leans closer for a better look. The Citizens react in horror

Primrose (*coming to the rescue*) I wouldn't get too close, if I were you. He/She has a highly contagious rash.
Slugslime (*leaping away from the child*) Ugh!

Act I, Scene 3   23

The others conceal their amusement

Slugslime (*to Tom*) Go and find your mother and those other miscreants!
Tom Certainly.
Slugslime And don't return without them!
Tom Of course not. (*Unseen by Slugslime, he winks to the Citizens*)

The Citizens exit R

The child follows. Comic business as Slugslime gives him a wide berth as he/she walks past him

Tom and Primrose are about to follow the Citizens

Slugslime Not you, Princess. I wish to speak to you — alone.
Tom (*not liking this*) I don't think —
Primrose It's all right, Tom.
Tom Well ... Just call out if you need me.

With a suspicious look at Slugslime, Tom exits R

Primrose What do you want, Mr Slugslime?
Slugslime (*now very smarmy*) Oh, please ... (*He moves closer to her*) Call me Slither.
Primrose (*moving away*) I'd rather not. I have no desire to be on such familiar terms with you.
Slugslime That is a great shame. (*Moving to her*) Because *I* have a desire to be on familiar terms with *you*.
Primrose (*moving further away*) Kindly state your business and leave.
Slugslime (*moving to her*) It has always been my wish to take a wife.
Primrose Really? I should have thought taking a *bath* more appropriate.
Slugslime (*that hurt!*) Take care, Princess! Do not mock me! You may regret it!
Primrose I already regret being in your company. What is it you want?
Slugslime I am thinking of making you my wife.
Primrose (*aghast*) What? Your wife! How dare you!
Slugslime Do not be so haughty, Princess. Remember, you are no longer the ruling force in this kingdom. If you show me some affection you can have all the food you want. And more.
Primrose I would rather starve!

Slugslime (*advancing on her*) Perhaps a little kiss will help you change your mind.
Primrose (*backing away*) Keep away from me, you repulsive creature!

Slugslime seizes her by the wrist and pulls her towards him

Primrose (*struggling to get free*) Let go! Let go of me! (*Calling*) Tom! Tom!

Tom rushes on from R and pulls Slugslime away from Primrose. He hits Slugslime, sending him crashing to the floor

Tom (*putting his arms around Primrose*) Are you all right?
Primrose Yes ...
Slugslime (*sitting up*) You will pay dearly for that, Tom Thumb!
Tom (*to Primrose*) I think you'd better go back to the palace.
Primrose Tom, don't do anything you may regret.
Tom It's all right, darling. (*He kisses her cheek*) I'll join you later.

Tom takes Primrose to exit R, and she leaves

Slugslime clambers to his feet

Slugslime (*sneering*) So! That's how it is. Very cosy. Does her father know about this?
Tom (*moving to C*) That's none of your business. I'm warning you, Slugslime. If you go near her again I'll not just knock you down, I'll knock you into the middle of next week!
Slugslime Brave words indeed, my boastful young friend! But you are forgetting something! You are forgetting my *magical powers*! Ha! Ha! Ha! (*He moves to DL*)

The lighting becomes strange and eerie. Weird sounds fill the air and threatening music plays under

Slugslime (*raising his arms*) Imps and Demons!
Come to my assistance!
And make sure this fool offers no resistance!

The Demons spring on from R and L brandishing tridents and cackling fiendishly

Act I, Scene 3

The Demons advance on Tom. He backs away upstage, until he is up against the table. Laughing his evil laugh, Slugslime moves up and stands R of Tom. The Demons retreat to the sides where they crouch in readiness

Tom To upset me was a grave mistake.
Now sweet revenge I mean to take!
You'll soon have cause to cringe and cower,
When I unleash on you my magic power!
The use of magic is a cowardly plan.
Why don't you fight me, man to man?
Don't hide behind your spells and chants.
Let me kick you in the pants!

Slugslime Tom Thumb, you are a boastful brat!
Now what can I do to remedy that?
I know! Your name itself gives inspiration!
Prepare yourself for a transformation!

Slugslime raises his arms and calls upon the forces of evil

Powers of darkness I summon thee!
Come aid my work in sorcery!
This meddlesome fool I mean to tame,
Make him live down to his stupid name!
Shrink and reduce this upstart scum!
Make him no bigger — than a thumb!
(*He makes magic pass at Tom*) *ATMAZOOM!!*

There is a flash, followed by a complete Black-out. The weird sounds and music become louder

Slugslime laughs and the Demons cackle

  Tom exits

Lighting returns to the previous eerie setting. The weird sounds and music decrease in volume. A spotlight illuminates the basket on the table

Slugslime and the Demons watch the basket with eager anticipation. Very slowly, a thumb-size version of Tom appears from inside the basket! (DON'T PANIC! See Production Notes.) Tiny "Tom" wiggles about

Slugslime Ha! Ha! Ha!
How do you like that, you little worm?
I told you I would make you squirm!
Now you're the size of a single digit,
All you can do is wiggle and fidget!

Slugslime comes forward with the Demons and addresses the audience

I've knocked that meddler down to size.
To challenge me was most unwise.
And if *you* lot give me any trouble,
I will reduce you all to a pile of rubble!
Ha! Ha! Ha!

Laughing his evil laugh, Slugslime sweeps out R

Snarling at the audience, the Demons follow him out

The lighting returns to normal, but the spotlight on the basket remains. The weird sounds and music fade out

"Tom" slowly sinks out of sight into the basket

A short pause

Mum Thumb's head appears around a side flat on L

Mum (*to audience*) Hallo!
Lucy (*her head appearing below Mum's*) Hallo!
Tim (*his head appearing below Lucy's*) Hallo!
Mum Has old Slimy gone, kids?
Audience Yes!

Mum, Tim and Lucy emerge

Tim Looks like we grasped through his slip again, Mum.
Mum Yes ... Hey! Where's Tom?

Mum, Tim and Lucy are all facing front. Their positioning must not obscure the audience's view of the basket

"Tom" pops up in the basket and wiggles about

Act I, Scene 3

Mum (*to audience*) Have you seen him, folks? Have you seen Tom?
Audience He's behind you!

Quickly "Tom" drops out of sight into the basket. Mum and the others turn to look upstage. As they turn to face front again, "Tom" pops up and wiggles about

Mum
Lucy   } (*together, to audience*) Oh, no he isn't!
Tim
Audience Oh, yes, he is!

While Mum and Lucy continue the exchange with the audience, Tim looks upstage. He sees "Tom", and does a huge double take. He lets out a strangled yell and staggers to one side of the stage

Lucy (*as she and Mum rush to him*) Timmy! What's the matter?
Tim (*gibbering*) I ... I ... I ...
Mum It's the lack of food! He's suffering from malformation! (*Shaking Tim*) Come on! Snap out of it! What are you tryin' to say?

Tim points upstage. Mum and Lucy look. "Tom" wiggles about. Mum and Lucy scream and huddle with Tim in a frightened group

Lucy W—w—what is it?
Mum I think it's a snake! (*To Tim*) You're the nearest thing we've got to a man! Go and get rid of it! (*Pushing him*) Go on!

Tim nervously approaches the table. "Tom" wiggles

Mum Is it a snake?
Tim No! It's — It's — *a tiny man!*
Mum
Lucy   } (*together*) A tiny man?!
Tim (*peering closer*) And you're never gonna believe this ...! I think it's — *Tom!*
Mum *Tom!*

Mum and Lucy rush up to join Tim at the table

Don't talk rubbish! Out the way! How can it be Tom? (*She peers at the little figure*)

"Tom" wiggles about

> (*Letting out a yell*) Ahhgh! IT IS TOM!! I'd recognize that dimple anywhere! Oh, Tom, my lovely lad! What's happened to you?! Oooo!!
>
> **Lucy** Shh! Listen! I think he's speaking!
> **Mum** What is it, Tom? Tell Mummy. (*She bends and puts her ear close to "Tom"*) Yes ... Yes ... He did *what*?! ... Oh, the rotten rotter!
> **Tim** What does he say?
> **Lucy** How did it happen?
> **Mum** It was that Slugslime! He put a magic spell on Tom and shrunk his assets!
> **Lucy** What are we going to do?
> **Mum** I dunno! He can't stay like that! He'll stick out like a sore thumb! Oh, what am I saying!
> **Lucy** Perhaps the king can help.
> **Mum** You're right! (*To "Tom"*) Don't worry, my little soldier. Mummy's gonna sort things out. (*To others*) Come on! Let's get him to the palace.

Mum, Tim and Lucy move in front of the table, thus obscuring their actions from the audience

> Careful! Careful! Don't squeeze him! Gently does it!

They are thus engaged as the Lights fade to Black-out

Music plays to cover the scene change, then the Lights come up on —

Scene 4

The lane (as Act I, Scene 2)

Laughing his evil laugh, Slugslime enters DL. *He is met with the usual barrage of abuse from the audience*

Slugslime Ha! Ha! Ha! That's Tom Thumb taken care of! I certainly knocked that young upstart down to size! He won't stand between me and the Princess anymore! And if he does, I will just stamp on him! Like that! (*He stamps his foot and laughs with evil relish*) Ha! Ha! Ha! Now you see how awesome my magical powers are. So be afraid!

Be very *very* afraid! I may decide to unleash them on you! Oh, yes I will!

"Oh, no, you won't!/Oh, yes, I will!" routine with Audience

Bah! You're not worth wasting my breath on! (*Moves to exit* DR) I'm going now.
Audience Good!
Slugslime But I'm watching you! (*To someone*) Especially *you!*

Snarling at them, he exits DR

Mum, Tim and Lucy enter from DL. *Mum is cradling a small basket in her arms (See Production Notes)*

Mum (*greeting the audience*) Hallo, folks! Hi, kids! We're on our way to the palace to see if the king can help poor Tom. He's in this basket. (*Getting weepy*) Oh, my poor boy! What's to become of him? Is he to spend the rest of his life getting lost down the back of the sofa? Or fighting with the hamster over who shall have use of the wheel? Ooo! (*Starts to cry*) Boo hoo!
Tim Steady, Mum! You'll drown him!
Mum Oh! I forgot! Silly me! (*To "Tom" in basket*) Sorry about that, Tom. (*To audience*) He's had one shower this month already. What's that, Tom? (*She puts her ear close to the basket and listens. To Audience*) He wants to know who I'm talking to. (*To "Tom"*) It's our friends out there. They're a nice crowd. Even the ones from (*local place*). D'you want to pop out and say hallo? (*Ear to basket and listens*) No? (*To audience*) He's a bit shy and nervous. Why don't you call out "Hallo, Tom"? Then he'll know you're friendly and he might come out. Give it a try. Go on.
Audience Hallo, Tom!

They look at the basket and nothing happens

Tim (*to audience*) Try again.
Audience Hallo, Tom!

Very slowly "Tom" appears from inside the basket

Mum Ah! There he is!

"Tom" quickly disappears from sight again

Oh, there he isn't!
Lucy I know. Why don't we get our friends out there to sing a nice song? That way Tom'll know there's nothing to be scared about.
Tim Yeah! A song! That's a brilliant idea, Lucy! Something like —— (*He gives a very loud and very off-key rendering of a current song*)
Mum *Whoa!* Put a sock in it! That's no good. That'd scare off (*current nasty*), that would! No, we want something nice and friendly. (*To Conductor/Pianist*) Have you got any ideas, Mr/Mrs Lloyd Webber?
Conductor/Pianist What about (*chosen song*)?
Lucy Oh, yes! That's a good one. Everybody knows that. (*To audience*) You can sing that one, can't you?

There will be those who will disagree!

Mum (*to audience*) Oh, yes, you can! You're born singists! I've heard some of you outside the (*local pub/club*) on Saturday nights. Now, we'll start it off, and you can all join in. (*To Conductor/Pianist*) Right! Handbrake off, dear!

The house lights come up

Song 7

Mum, Lucy and Tim sing and encourage the audience to join in. During the number, "Tom" appears from the basket. When this happens Tim starts singing very loudly causing "Tom" to disappear again. This business is repeated a few times. Finally, "Tom" remains in view, and even wiggles about in time to the music

When the song ends, the house lights go down

Mum (*to "Tom"*) There you are, my little soldier. They're a lovely crowd, aren't they?

"Tom" nods

(*To audience*) Thanks, folks! (*Ear close to "Tom"*) What's that? (*To audience*) Tom wants to thank you, as well.

Mum comes forward and "Tom" nods to all parts of the house

Thanks again, folks. Bye! Say goodbye, Tom.

"Tom" wiggles about

Act I, Scene 5

Mum exits DR, *followed by Lucy*

Tim (*to audience*) I still think it would have been better if we'd sung —— (*He does his loud off-key rendering again*)

Lucy re-enters from DR. *She grabs Tim by the ear and drags him out*

The Lights fade to Black-out

Music is played to cover the scene change

Scene 5

Throne Room of the palace

Full set. Stone walls adorned with flags and shields, etc. Against the right wings is a throne. In the centre of the back wall is an arched window, behind which a backcloth or cyclorama depicting the view outside the palace (See Production Notes) Entrances R *and* L

The Lights come up on an empty stage

The King pops his head out from R, *and then creeps cautiously on*

Looking furtively about him, he takes a bag of jelly babies from his pocket. He is about to pop one in his mouth when he catches sight of the audience

King Oh, I say! I didn't realize you were there. You won't say anything about this, will you? This is my secret supply of jelly babies. Since that wretched giant came, these are all I've had to eat. I'd love to offer you one, but I'm afraid there aren't many left. You won't tell that awful Slugslime, will you?
Audience No.
King Jolly good show.

He puts the sweet in his mouth and chews blissfully

Slugslime enters suddenly from L

Slugslime Ah! There you are!

The King chokes on his sweet

Slugslime What is it? Is something up?
King (*after a big swallow*) Not anymore! What are you doing here? Apart from making the place look untidy!
Slugslime There is something you should know.
King Has the giant decided to go on a diet?
Slugslime This does not concern my master. (*Moving closer to the King*) It is something of a very personal nature.
King Well, they say (*popular deodorant*) is very good. But in your case I'd try "Harpic".
Slugslime (*snarling*) Do not be flippant with me! Remember who I am and *what* I am!
King Oh, I know what *you* are, all right!
Slugslime It concerns the princess. Your daughter. Primrose.
King Yes, I do know her name. What about her?
Slugslime She has taken my fancy.
King Nonsense! Primrose is a very well brought-up girl. She'd never take anything that didn't belong to her.
Slugslime I mean she has caught my eye.
King Oh! Which one?
Slugslime I want her for my wife.
King But what does your wife want with my Primrose?
Slugslime (*exasperated*) Listen to me, you silly old fool! I intend to marry your daughter!
King Marry my ... Oh, I say! Does she know about this?
Slugslime I have mentioned it, yes.
King And what did she say?
Slugslime At the moment she is undecided. (*Sneering*) But it is only a matter of time before she consents. I can be *very* persuasive.
King Well, I must say this has come as a surprise. I had no idea you and she were ... er ... I thought she hated the sight of you just like everyone else.

Primrose enters from L

King Ah! Primrose! (*Going to her*) Is this true?
Primrose Is what true, Father?
King That you are thinking of marrying this reject from (*current TV or monster movie*)?
Primrose Did he tell you that?
Slugslime I thought it only right to inform your father of my intentions.

Act I, Scene 5

Primrose And now I will inform him of *my* intentions. I will never marry that obnoxious, loathsome and thoroughly repulsive creature! I would rather become a (*local rival football team*) supporter!
King (*to Slugslime*) I think you can take that as a no.
Primrose There is only one person I shall ever marry.
King That's right ... What?
Primrose Father, the time has come for you to learn the truth. I have fallen in love with someone. Someone you know very well and hold in high esteem.
King It's not (*name of local personality can be used*) is it?
Primrose No. It is Tom Thumb!
King My head gardener!
Primrose We have been in love for a long time but we lacked the courage to tell you of our true feelings for one another.
King But my dear ... He's a commoner ...
Slugslime (*to King*) You need not concern yourself with Tom Thumb. He is no longer a *big* issue.
Primrose What do you mean?
Slugslime (*sneering*) You'll find out, Princess, you'll find out! Ha! Ha! Ha!

Laughing his evil laugh, Slugslime exits R

King (*sitting on the throne*) Primrose, you know I think the world of young Tom, but he is hardly the right choice for the husband of a royal princess.
Primrose (*going to him*) But, Father, we love each other.
King Are you sure, m'dear?
Primrose I've never been more sure of anything in my life.

Song 8

Illuminated by a romantic spotlight, Primrose expresses her love in song

King (*rising and putting his arm around Primrose*) Well, m'dear. You do have it badly. And if Tom feels the same way about you as you do about him...
Primrose Oh, he does! He does!
King Then why should we let old-fashioned ideals and customs stand in the way. You have my blessing. Both of you.
Primrose (*overjoyed and hugging him*) Oh, Father! Thank you! Thank you!

Mum Thumb, Tim and Lucy enter from L. *Mum still cradles the basket. They are followed by the Citizens, who fill the back and sides of the stage*

Mum Sorry to barge in like this, Your Mint Imperials, but we've got a *big* problem. Well, it's not so much a *big* problem as a *little* problem. Let's call it a *big little* problem. What I mean is —
King Mum Thumb, what are you babbling about?
Tim It's Tom!
Primrose (*alarmed*) What's happened to Tom? Where is he?
Mum He's right here.
Primrose (*looking about*) Where?
Mum Hold on to yer crowns. He's in this basket.
King Have you been at the special brew again?
Mum It's true! (*To basket*) Come on! It's time to show yourself!

"Tom" rises from the basket. Reaction from the King, Primrose and the Citizens

King By Jove! It's a tiny little chap!
Mum It's Tom.
Primrose It ... it can't be! It can't be Tom!
Mum It's him all right. Take a closer look.

Primrose bends forward to look. "Tom" wiggles about

Primrose (*staggering back*) Tom! It *is* Tom! ... Oh, Tom! (*She buries her face in her hands*)
King But ... How did this happen? ... How did he get so small?
Mum Well, he didn't shrink in the wash! It was that nasty Slugslime!
Tim He put a magic spell on him.
Primrose (*to "Tom"*) Oh, Tom! Why did this have to happen now? I've just told my father that we love each other! And he's given us his blessing.

"Tom" wiggles about excitedly

Mum Eh? What's this? Y'mean, you and our Tom ... (*To "Tom"*) Tom Thumb! You kept that quiet, you little tinker, you!
King But this alters everything.
Primrose What do you mean, Father?
King Well ... I can hardly have a son-in-law so ... er ... titchy.
Lucy It won't be much fun for the princess either!

Act I, Scene 5   35

King Quite, quite. What on earth is to be done about it?
Mum That's why we're here, Your Royal Jelly. We thought *you* might help.
Tim We thought you might be able to remove the spell.
King But I don't know anything about magic. I can do a few card tricks, but that's as far as it goes.
Primrose Wait a minute! Why not try Spellena?
Mum Is that on prescription?
Primrose Spellena is a witch. (*To King*) Perhaps she can remove the spell.
King True. It's worth a try. But from what I've heard she's a very disagreeable old crone.
Mum Oh, I'll soon sort her out. I'm used to dealing with old crones. I'm not a member of the (*local WI*) for nothin'! Where do we find this witch?
King She dwells in the depths of the Weird Wood. It's not a very pleasant place. Especially after dark.
Tim (*quivering*) Oh, no! I might have known! The Weird Wood! Why can't she live in (*local sheltered housing*)?
Mum (*to "Tom"*) Right, let's find this old witch and get you sorted out. What's that? (*She puts her ear close to "Tom"*) Oh! (*To Primrose*) He wants to speak to you, Your Royal Icing.

Primrose puts her ear close to "Tom" and listens

Mum (*to the others*) Oy! Where's yer manners? Give 'em some privacy.

They all look the other way

Primrose Yes ... yes ... And I love you too, Tom.
All (*to audience*) Ahhh!

Primrose kisses "Tom". He wiggles about, excitedly

Mum (*to all*) Well, here we go! Wish us luck!
Others Good luck!
Mum (*to audience*) That includes you, folks!
Audience Good luck!
Tim (*to audience*) We'll need it!
Mum (*to Tim and Lucy*) Come on, Batman and Robin! (*or other duo*) Let's go and find that witch!

Mum, Tim and Lucy exit R, *waving goodbye to the others and the audience*

Primrose Oh, my poor Tom. Do you really think the witch will be able to help him?
King Let us hope so, m'dear, let us hope so.

Slugslime enters from R

Slugslime Ha! Ha! Ha!
Primrose (*about to spring at him*) *You!!*
King (*restraining her*) Steady, Primrose.
Slugslime (*sneering*) I see from your anger that you have discovered the fate of Tom Thumb. How do you like the pocket-size version? Very handy, eh? Ha! Ha! Ha!
Primrose Laugh all you want, you vile monster! Soon your evil spell will be removed.
King Yes! At this very moment help is being sought from Spellena, the witch.
Slugslime (*snarling with contempt*) Pah! Spellena, the witch! She is no match for *my* magic. There is no one alive who can undo one of *my* spells! (*Becoming oily again*) But I have returned on a different matter. The giant, being a very thoughtful and caring employer, is much displeased at your refusal to marry me. So much so that he thinks you should be removed from here and take up residence in his castle.
Primrose (*aghast*) What?!
Slugslime He feels that it will give you and I a chance to become better acquainted. And I agree with him.
Primrose Never! (*Clinging to the King*) Father...
King (*to Slugslime*) You can't take my daughter away from me! I will not allow it!
Slugslime (*snarling*) You have no choice in the matter, old man! (*To Primrose*) I could of course use my magic powers to transport you to the giant's castle, but my master has very kindly offered to come and fetch you personally.

Horrified reaction from all the others

King You mean the giant is coming *here*?
Slugslime Oh, yes! He should arrive at any moment. Ah! Listen! Here he comes now!

Act I, Scene 5   37

We hear the sound of the Giant's huge and heavy footsteps approaching. (See Production Notes for the whole of the Giant sequence). They reverberate around the stage and auditorium. Suitable threatening music plays under, and continues until the end of the Act. At the same time, the lighting takes on an unearthly glow

The frightened Citizens retreat to the sides and cower in terrified groups. The King and Primrose move to a downstage corner. Slugslime is on the opposite side, revelling in fiendish glee

Finally, the footsteps come to a halt

The booming laughter and voice of the Giant fills the stage and auditorium

Giant   (*bellowing*) HO! HO! HO!
             Beware you puny mortals, for I am here!
             I hope you are shaking with dread and fear!
             With one mighty breath I can blow these walls down.
             With one mighty stamp I can flatten your town!
             HO! HO! HO!

There are cries and screams as the Giant's enormous eye appears at the window (See Production Notes). It is illuminated by an eerie spotlight

Slugslime Ha! Ha! Ha! (*Turning and bowing to the eye*) Welcome, Master, welcome!
Giant   Slugslime, you are my faithful slave.
             Which of these females do you crave?
             Point out the one you hope to marry.
             And she to my castle I will carry!

Slugslime (*pointing to Primrose*) There she is!
King (*standing in front of Primrose, protectively*) You can't do this! I forbid it!

Snarling, Slugslime seizes the King and roughly pushes him away to the other side of the stage

Primrose (*moving nearer to C*) Father...!

Behind Primrose, the huge hand of the Giant slides on from the side (See Production Notes)

The Citizens shriek and cry

King Primrose! *Look out!*
Citizens (*and no doubt, the audience!*) Behind you!

Primrose turns and sees the monstrous hand inching towards her. She lets out a scream and backs away. Slugslime grabs her and forces her into the grasp of the Giant's hand. The huge fingers close around her

Primrose (*struggling to get free*) Let me go! Help me! *Help!*
Giant HO! HO! HO!

Holding the struggling Primrose, the Giant's hand slides out the way it came in

King Primrose! Primrose!

The Giant's eye disappears from the window. The lighting returns to previous setting

Slugslime (*to the audience*) Now she is mine! *All mine! Ha! Ha! Ha!*

Laughing his evil laugh, Slugslime sweeps out

The Citizens rush up to the window and look out. The King sinks on to the throne and buries his face in his hands. Dramatic music up to full, as —

—*the* CURTAIN *falls*

ACT II

Scene 1

The Weird Wood

Full set. The backcloth and side wings represent trees and foliage. UL, *the front of a small thatched cottage with a practical door is seen. The Wood should be in no way sinister-looking. Entrances* R *and* L

When the CURTAIN *rises, the stage is empty and bathed in dappled sunlight*

To suitable music, Birds, Butterflies and small animal Wildlife enter from various directions. They go into their dance, ending in a tableau

Song 9

Mum (*off* R, *calling*) *Yoo hoo!* Anyone at home?

The Wildlife scatters and exits in various directions

Mum Thumb, still carrying the basket, creeps on from R. *She beckons, and Tim and Lucy enter, holding hands and looking very nervous*

They all gaze about and are surprised at the tranquillity of their surroundings

Tim Is this it? Is this the Weird Wood?
Lucy I suppose it must be. It's not a bit like I expected.
Tim Same here. I thought it was going be really *scary* and *spooky*.
Mum This is more like (*reference to local park or play area*), without the (*reference to suit*)!

They continue to gaze about. Tim catches sight of the audience and lets out a loud yell. Mum and Lucy jump with fright

Mum Don't *do* that! Oh! Me whole life flashed before me! All twenty-five years of it!

Tim Look! Our mates are here! (*Waving to audience*) Hallo, folks!

Mum and Lucy wave and greet the audience

Mum Well, it must be all right if you're here, folks. Apart from Timmy, have you seen anything odd or strange?
Audience No.
Lucy It looks a very nice place. I can't imagine an old witch living here.
Tim No. I wonder why they call it the *Weird* Wood?
Mum (*suddenly alarmed and pointing to* L) That's why!

A crone-like woman enters from L. *She looks like the classic witch of fairytales*

Mum and the others retreat to stage R. *Muttering to herself, the Crone moves up to the cottage and knocks on the door*

Lucy Do you think that's her?
Tim Do you think she's the witch, Mum?
Mum Well, it's too tall for Anne Robinson! Go and ask her!
Tim (*squirming*) Me?!
Mum What are you? A man or a mouse?
Tim If we still had that cheese, I'd show you.
Mum (*giving him a push*) Go on!

Tim nervously approaches the Crone

Tim Er ... excuse me ...
Crone (*turning with a snarl*) What is it?
Tim (*reacting*) Aggh!
Crone Well?
Tim Er ... Lovely year we're having for the time of weather ... er ...
Crone What do you want?
Tim Are you the ditch ... I mean, the switch ... I mean, the snitch ... I mean ...
Crone Stop wasting my time! What is it you want? (*Advancing on him*) Eh? Eh?
Tim (*a desperate wail*) MUM!!

Mum and Lucy move across

Mum (*putting on a big smile*) Hallo!

Act II, Scene 1

Lucy (*doing the same*) Hallo!
Crone Crikey! It's Ant and Dec! (*Or other duo*) Who are you?
Mum I'm his mother.
Crone That figures. What is it you want? Out with it! I'm a very busy woman!
Mum Oh, I'm sure you are. I expect you've got a couple of cauldrons on the bubble.
Crone What?
Lucy We've come to ask for your help.
Tim Yes. Can you make something that's small grow big again?
Crone I beg your pardon! (*To Mum*) 'Ere! You want to have a word with him.
Mum He's in the basket.
Crone He ought to be in a home!
Mum Not him! My other son, Tom.
Crone Tom?
Mum Yes. He's in this basket because he's only the size of a thumb.
Crone (*utterly confused*) Only the size of a ... Are you lot supposed to be out on your own? Look, why don't you try going out and coming in again. Better still — (*snarling at them*) *don't come in at all!*

The door of the cottage opens and Spellena comes out. She is young and very pretty

Spellena (*with a radiant smile*) Good-afternoon.
Crone (*turning to her*) Ah! There you are. About time too. I've come for the magic potion. The "all warts gone in ten minutes guaranteed" potion. You said it'd be ready this afternoon.
Spellena That's right. Here it is. (*She takes a small packet from her apron pocket and hands it to the Crone*)
Crone And you're sure this'll get rid of all my warts?
Spellena Yes, without fail.
Crone Even the ones...? (*She whispers in Spellena's ear*)
Spellena Yes, even those. Just make sure you read the instructions on the packet very carefully.
Crone Right! (*Peering at packet*) May contain eye of newt. Oh, I can't wait to try it out! Wart free after all these years! I'm off to (*local club*) tonight! So, look out, boys, here I come! Hee! Hee! Hee! (*Chuckling, she moves to the exit* L. *She stops and waves the packet at Spellena*) Thanks, Spellena!

She exits L

Mum and the others react

Mum Did she call you Spellena?
Spellena That's right.
Tim (*incredulously*) Are *you* the witch?
Spellena I am.
Mum And *she's* not a witch?
Spellena No. She works on the checkout at (*local supermarket*).
Mum I thought I recognized her polite smile!
Lucy But we expected you to be an ugly old crone like her.
Tim There's nothing ugly or crony about you.
Spellena Well, what's the point of having magical powers if you can't use them on yourself? I'll let you into a secret. I'm really a hundred and fifty years old. (*She does a twirl*) Not bad, eh?
Mum Get down to Boots, dear! You'll make a fortune!
Spellena So, how can I help you?
Tim (*ogling her*) Cor! In lots of ways!

Lucy gives him a sharp nudge

Mum It's my son Tom. He's in this basket.
Spellena All of him?
Mum He had a spell put on him. He's been shrunk to the size of a thumb!
Lucy It was Slugslime, the giant's henchman, who did it.
Spellena Ah, yes. I have heard of him. A very unpleasant individual. He gives the art of sorcery a bad name.
Mum Well, do you think you can help our Tom?
Spellena I'd better have a look at him first.
Mum (*looking in basket*) Tom? ... Tom? (*To Spellena*) I think he's dozed off. (*Shaking the basket*) Wakey, wakey Tom!

"Tom" rises from the basket

Mum There he is! (*To "Tom"*) Tom, this is Spellena. She's the nice lady who's gonna make you all better.
Spellena (*leaning forward*) Hallo, Tom. It's lovely to meet you.

"Tom" wiggles about

Mum You'll have to forgive him. He's a bit *short* on conversation. (*To "Tom"*) What's that? (*She puts her ear to "Tom"*) Yes ... yes. (*To Spellena*) He says you're very pretty for a witch.
Spellena Thank you, Tom.

Act II, Scene 2

Mum (*aside to her*) We won't tell him how old you really are. The poor lad's got enough to cope with. Well, do you think you can make him full size again?
Spellena Oh, yes. There shouldn't be any problem.
Tim What do *we* have to do?
Spellena Just remain inaudible.
Tim Oh, Right! (*Dumbly*) Wot?
Mum In other words — keep yer cakehole shut!
Spellena Just give me a few seconds to remember the spell correctly. (*She puts her hands to her forehead and mumbles to herself*) Yes. That's it. Now I'm ready!

Positions at this point should be: Mum with basket c. *Spellena* lc. *Tim and Lucy* r

The lighting becomes magical. Suitable music plays under

Spellena I summon the powers of goodness and light.
Banish all evil and make things come right.
Remove the spell that has shrunk young Tom Thumb,
And return him to normal for his friends and his mum!
(*She makes a magic pass at "Tom"*)

There is a flash, followed by a complete Black-out. Music up to full. Magical sounds fill the air

Mum drops the basket

Tom enters and jumps into Mum's arms

The lighting returns to the previous setting. The music and sounds fade out

Tom Hallo, everybody!
Mum (*dropping him to his feet*) She did it! You're back to normal! Oh, Tom! Come 'ere! (*She hugs Tom*)

Tom goes and hugs Tim and Lucy. Tim picks up the basket

Mum Oy! Where's your manners? Aren't you gonna thank the lady responsible?
Tom Of course I am. (*He goes to Spellena, holding out his hand to her*) Thank you, Spellena.

Spellena (*taking his hand, a little flirtatious*) There's no need for thanks, Tom. It was my pleasure to restore such a fine, handsome young man to his proper proportions.
Mum (*aside to Spellena*) Hands off, Granny. He's already spoken for. (*Aside to Tom*) Don't be fooled, son. She's not what she seems. Besides, you'll make the princess jealous.
Tom Primrose! Oh, I can't wait to show her that I'm back to normal. She loves me and her father has given us his blessing! Things couldn't be any better!

Song 10

Tom leads Lucy, Tim, Mum and Spellena in a joyful song and dance

The Wildlife enters to participate in the merriment

The number ends with Tom and the others exiting R, *waving goodbye to Spellena, as the Lights fade to Black-out*

Music to cover the scene change, and then the Lights come up on —

SCENE 2

The lane (as Act I, Scene 2)

A jubilant Crone (minus warts) skips on from DL

Crone (*to audience*) Hallo! I bet you didn't recognize me! (*Showing off her wart-free face*) Look! Look! The magic potion worked! All my warts have gone in ten minutes! Just like it said on the packet! (*Ecstatically*) Ooh! I'm beautiful again! All I need now is a fella to take me to (*local club*) tonight. (*To audience*) Any offers? (*By-play with audience*) Oh, please yerselves! You don't know what you're missing!

Slugslime enters from DR. *He keeps his back to the Crone*

Ah! There's a man! (*Peering across*) At least ... I *think* it's a man. I'll give him a try anyway. (*She preens herself, and then slinks across to Slugslime. In a seductive voice*) Hi there.
Slugslime (*turning to face her*) Yes?
Crone (*reacting with a cry of horror*) Waagah!!

Act II, Scene 2   45

Slugslime What do you want?
Crone Certainly not *you*! Forget it! (*To audience*) He needs that potion more than I do! I'll try me luck in (*local place*). (*She moves to exit* DR, *and then looks back at Slugslime*) Yuck!

The Crone exits

Slugslime (*snarling at the audience*) Grr! So! You are still here, are you? I thought there was a funny smell! Grr! (*By-play with audience*) Well, even the sight of your ugly faces can't spoil my happy mood. With Princess Primrose safely locked up in the giant's castle, I have her all to myself! Very soon I will force her to become my wife! And there is no one who can stop me, is there?
Audience Oh, yes, there is!
Slugslime Oh, no, there isn't!
Audience Oh, yes, there is!
Slugslime Oh, no, there isn't!
Audience Oh, yes, there is!
Slugslime Who?
Audience Tom Thumb!
Slugslime (*with scorn*) Pah! Tom Thumb! What can that little squirt do? He's only two inches tall!
Audience Oh, no, he's not! Not now! (*Etc, etc!*)
Slugslime *What*?! Are you telling me ... or *should* be telling me ... that my magic spell on Tom Thumb has been removed?
Audience Yes!
Slugslime (*enraged*) Who has dared to do this thing?
Audience Spellena! The witch!
Slugslime Grr! Curse upon curse! This is very annoying!
Audience Good!
Slugslime (*sneering*) But it will make no difference to my plans! Tom Thumb will never see the princess again! *Never*! Ha! Ha! Ha!

Laughing his evil laugh, he sweeps out DR

Mum, Tom, Tim and Lucy enter from DL. *They all greet the audience*

Mum Oh, folks, it's so lovely having my Tom back to normal. (*To someone*) I bet you missed seeing him full size as well, didn't you? (*Indicating Tom's legs*) I wonder why? Oh, he's my handsome, strapping son again! (*She hugs Tom*)
Tim Hey! What about *me*?
Mum What about you?

Tim Aren't I your handsome, strapping son as well?
Mum You're not so much strappin' as overlappin'.
Lucy You'll always be handsome and strapping to me! (*Cuddling him*) Oh, Timmy!
Tim (*all soppy*) Oh, Lucy!
Mum Oh, put a sock in it! What do you think this is, (*TV programme*)?

The 1st and 2nd Citizens enter from DR

Mum (*to them*) Hey, look! Our Tom's back to normal!
2nd Citizen Congratulations, Tom.
Tom Thanks. (*To Mum*) Can we get on to the palace now? I'm dying to see Primrose.
1st Citizen (*as gloomy as ever*) She's not there.
Tom What?
1st Citizen I said, she's not there. She's in the giant's castle.

Reaction from Tom and the others

Tom What are you talking about?
2nd Citizen After you left, the giant came and took the Princess away to his castle. He's got her locked up there. It was all Slugslime's doing.
Others Oh, no!
1st Citizen And that's not the worst part.
2nd Citizen Slugslime is planning to marry her!
Others (*aghast*) Marry her?!

Tom strides towards the exit DL

Mum Tom! Where are you going?
Tom Where do you think I'm going? I'm going to the giant's castle! I've got to get Primrose out of there!
1st Citizen You're wasting your time.
2nd Citizen The castle is too well guarded. You'll never get in.
Tom I must try!
Mum (*going to him*) They're right, Tom. It's hopeless.
Tom There must be a way. I can't leave my darling Primrose in that monster's clutches. I love her far too much.

Song 10a (Reprise of Song 2)

The general lighting fades, and Tom is illuminated by a spotlight as he sings

Act II, Scene 3

Mum, Tim, Lucy and Citizens exit quietly

After the number, the spotlight slowly fades on Tom. Black-out

Music to cover the scene change, and then the Lights come up on —

Scene 3

The Royal Gardens (as Act I, Scene 1)

The King is discovered seated on the top step in a very despondent mood. The Citizens are trying their best to cheer him up with a song and dance

Song 11

King (*standing up*) My loyal subjects, I thank you for that splendid attempt at trying to cheer me. But I am afraid there is nothing that can dispel my melancholy. The thought of my only daughter imprisoned in the giant's castle is more than I can bear. Oh, my poor Primrose! (*He weeps into a large handkerchief*)

Some of the Citizens and Children share his tears

Mum, Tim and Lucy enter from L. Tim is carrying the basket

Mum Crikey! Don't tell me they've cancelled (*TV soap or something topical*)?
Lucy I think they're upset because of the princess.
Mum I know that, you chump. I was just trying to lighten the mood. Hallo, Your Maj. We're ever so sorry to hear about the princess.
King (*coming down to her*) Thank you, Mum Thumb.
Mum But I've got something that'll cheer you up a bit. (*She points to* L) Look who's here!

Tom enters from L. The Citizens react

Tom (*crossing to King*) Your Majesty!
King (*shaking his hand*) Tom, my boy! I'm delighted to see you restored to normal. I only wish that Primrose were here to see it. She's been —
Tom Yes, we know. Your Majesty, there must be some way of getting into the Giant's castle.

Slugslime enters suddenly from R

Slugslime Oh, no there isn't, Tom Thumb! No one can enter the castle without *my* knowledge! So you can forget all about trying to rescue the Princess! (*Sneering*) She will remain there until the day she becomes my bride! Ha! Ha! Ha!
Tom I'll find some way of beating you, Slugslime!
Slugslime (*with mock terror*) Ooh! I'm shivering in my shoes! Ha! Ha! Ha! But I am here on a more important matter. The giant's cook has been suddenly taken ill.
Mum Huh! Food poisoning, I'll bet!
Slugslime Another must be found immediately. (*Moving to Mum*) I understand you are one of those.
Mum (*indignantly*) I beg your pardon!
Slugslime A cook!
King Mum Thumb is the palace cook.
Slugslime (*sneering*) Well, as you no longer have any food that needs cooking, she must be out of a job. (*To Mum*) You will report to the castle and take up your duties as cook to the giant.
Mum You what? I'm not gonna cook for that great big overgrown haystack!
Slugslime Oh, yes, you will!
Mum Oh, no, I won't!
Slugslime If you refuse I will show you the full extent of my magical powers!
Mum You can show me what you like! I'm not doin' it!
Slugslime (*snarling*) Very well! You asked for it! (*Calling up the evil forces*) Powers of darkness, I summon thee! Come aid my work in sorcery! Ha! Ha! Ha!

There are flashes of lightning and claps of thunder. The lighting becomes dark and eerie. Sinister music plays. The others react

Tim (*terrified*) You'd better do it, Mum!
Tom (*to her*) Yes! Remember what he did to me!
Mum You're right. I don't want miniaturizin' at my age! (*To Slugslime*) Whoa! Hold yer hexes! You win!
Slugslime (*sneering*) I thought so! (*Addressing the lightning and thunder*) CUT!!

The effects and music stop abruptly. The lighting returns to normal

Mum But I'm not going into that 'orrible castle on me own. I want immoral support.

Act II, Scene 3   49

Slugslime Oh, very well. (*Indicating Tim and Lucy*) Those two nitwits can go with you.
Tim (*with gloom*) Thanks a bunch, Mum!
Mum What about Tom?
Slugslime Oh, no! *Not him*! I don't want *him* anywhere near the castle. I don't trust him! Be at the giant's castle in ten minutes. (*He moves to exit* R, *and turns*) And don't be late! Don't make me have to come and fetch you!

He sweeps out R

Tim I wish you were coming with us, Tom.
Lucy Yes, then you could have found some way of rescuing the Princess.
Tom (*sighing sadly*) I might as well still be the size of a thumb for all the good I can do ... (*Suddenly struck by an idea*) Wait a minute! That's it!
Others What is?
Tom If I were *small* again you could easily smuggle me into the castle with you.
Mum That's a thought.
King It sounds a capital idea, Tom, but how are you going to achieve it? Slugslime is hardly likely to oblige by making you tiny again, is he?
Tom He won't have to. Spellena, the witch, reversed the spell. I'm sure she can re-reverse it.
Mum You're right! Quick! Let's get it done before old Slimy comes back!

They rush to exit L, *but pull up short as Spellena herself enters there*

Mum Crikey! That's lucky. We were just comin' to see you.
Spellena I know. I have been following events in my mirror.
Tim Cor! Have we made the front page?
Spellena My *magic* mirror.
Tim Oh! (*He guffaws*)
Mum You stupid boy!
Spellena (*to Tom*) You wish me to make you thumb-size again.
Tom Yes, please, if you can.
Spellena It will be the work of a second.
Tom Before you do, there is something I need to ask. Once inside the castle I mean to rescue Primrose. I may need to return to my normal size to achieve it.

Spellena I have anticipated that. There is a magic word that will instantly return you to your full size. All you have to do is say it. The magic word is — ALAKAZAM.
Mum Alakazam ... Alakazam. (*To audience*) Can you remember that, folks? (*Archly*) 'Cos you never know!
Tim (*to Mum*) Basket!
Mum Don't be so rude!
Tim No, you'll be needing this again. (*He hands her the basket*)
Spellena And now to make you tiny Tom Thumb once more.

The lighting becomes magical. Suitable music plays under. Magical sounds fill the air

> I summon the powers of light and the air.
> Help Tom find his princess in the giant's lair.
> For him to succeed and dangers overcome,
> Make him once more the size of a thumb!
> (*She makes magic pass at Tom*)

There is a flash, followed by a complete Black-out

The music and magical sounds become louder. These continue for a while, and then they fade out as The Lights come up on —

Scene 4

The lane (as Act I, Scene 2)

The Crone enters from DR

Crone (*to audience*) I didn't have any luck finding a fella in (*local place*). I just can't understand it. You'd think they'd be queuing up to take out a gorgeous-looking bird like me.

Song 12

This should be a comical rendering of something like "I Feel Pretty" from "West Side Story" (See copyright details)

> *During the number, a succession of male Citizens enter. In song, the Crone flirtatiously plays up to them and succeeds in frightening them away*

Act II, Scene 4

Finally, the King enters. He receives the same treatment and makes his escape

(*After song*) What a miserable lot! (*To someone in audience*) Are you sure you won't change your mind about taking me to (*local club*)? (*By-play with audience*) Oh, suit yerself! I'll see what I can find in (*another local place*). I've heard they've got some real men there!

She exits DL

Mum, Tim and Lucy creep on from DR. *Mum is cradling the basket*

They look cautiously about, and then greet the audience

Tim Hallo, folks! Hi, kids! Old Slimy isn't about, is he?
Audience No.
Lucy Are you sure?
Audience Yes.
Mum (*to basket*) You hear that, Tom? The coast's clear. You can come out now. (*"Tom" rises from the basket*)
Mum (*To "Tom"*) There's only our mates here. Do you want to give 'em a wave?

"Tom" nods and wiggles at the audience

Lucy We oughtn't to hang about. Remember what Slugslime said. If we're late he'll come looking for us!

Slugslime enters DL *and remains at the side*

The audience will be shouting warnings, but the others don't take any notice. "Tom" senses something is wrong and disappears into the basket

Slugslime Ah!
Mum
Lucy } (*together, seeing him and yelling*) Aghhh!!
Tim

Panic-stricken, they look at the basket and sigh with relief when they discover that Tom is out of sight

Slugslime (*crossing to them*) You're late! You should have been at the giant's castle five minutes ago.

Mum Why, what happened?
Slugslime Be warned! If my master's food is not on the table at the correct time he will be very, very angry!
Mum Ah! Diddums!
Slugslime And believe me, you don't want to see him when he gets angry.
Tim I don't want to see him at all!
Slugslime Hurry up! (*Moving to exit* DL) To the castle!

They are about to follow, when Slugslime stops and turns

Slugslime Wait! (*Moves to them*) Where is Tom Thumb?
Mum T ... T ... Tom *who*?
Slugslime Tom Thumb! Your other son.
Mum Oh! Er ... He's not here. (*To others*) Is he?
Tim
Lucy } (*together, shaking their heads*) No!
Slugslime *Where* is he?
Lucy He ... he was so upset about the princess he decided to emigrate.
Tim Yes. He's gone to (*local place*)!
Slugslime (*sneering*) The best place for him! He should be quite at home with all those other losers! I hope he never returns. Let's go!

He moves to exit DL. *The others are about to follow, when Slugslime stops and turns again*

Wait! (*Moves to them*) What have you got in that basket?
Mum Which basket?
Slugslime *That* basket!
Mum Oh, *this* basket! Nothin'!
Slugslime What are you carrying it for then?
Mum I ... I might find something to put in it.
Slugslime Like what?
Mum Er ... Eggs! Then I'll have all my eggs in one basket.
Slugslime Rubbish! You're hiding something! Let me see it!

He makes a grab for the basket. Suddenly, Lucy lets out a cry and points excitedly at the audience

Lucy Look! Look! I can't believe it! *Look*!
Slugslime (*looking towards the audience*) What is it?
Lucy It's Johnny Depp! (*Or another film/TV personality*) (*Waving, madly*) Hallo, Johnny!

Act II, Scene 5   53

Slugslime You fool! That's not Johnny Depp! What would he be doing in a dump like this?
Lucy No, you're right. It's not him. It's (*another media personality*)! (*Waving, madly*) Hallo, (*name*)!

Slugslime peers out at the audience

Mum (*aside to Lucy*) Have you gone bonkers?
Lucy (*aside*) I'm trying to keep him away from the basket.
Mum Oh, I get it! You're creating a nasturtium. (*Going to Slugslime*) And look — (*pointing*) Isn't that (*another media personality*), over there? (*Waving*) Hallo, (*name*)!
Slugslime (*snarling*) Stop this nonsense! We have wasted enough time! To the castle!

Slugslime exits DL, *followed by Mum and Lucy*

Tim lingers, still peering out at the audience

Tim Hallo (*name of personality*)! I'm one of your biggest fans. Can I come down and get your autograph?

Lucy re-enters and drags Tim out DL. *He is still calling and waving to the personality, as the Lights fade to Black-out*

Music to cover the scene change, and then the Lights come up on —

Scene 5

Kitchen of the Giant's castle

Full set. The backcloth and side wings are painted to represent the kitchen with everything on a large scale. Plates, knife and fork, spoon, sauce bottle, salt and pepper pots, etc. Also painted on the scenery is a big portrait of the giant himself in all his bearded beastliness. There is a practical table at the back covered by a cloth that reaches the ground. On the table is a large mixing bowl, rolling pin and other cooking paraphernalia. Entrances R *and* L

To suitable music, the Children, as kitchen staff, march on. They are dressed as cooks and kitchen maids. They form a line across the back and face front

The music ends

Princess Primrose enters from R. *She is flanked by two Guards*

1ˢᵗ Guard That's your exercise over for today, Princess. Now it's time to go back to your nice comfy cell.
Primrose You have no right to keep me imprisoned here.
1ˢᵗ Guard T'ain't nothin' to do wiv us. We're only obeyin' orders.
2ⁿᵈ Guard Yeah. An' horders his horders — horders his.
Primrose If you take me back to the palace, the king will reward you handsomely.
1ˢᵗ Guard Are you 'avin' a laugh?
2ⁿᵈ Guard She mus' fink we're stoopid.
1ˢᵗ Guard If we did that, wot d'you think Slugslime and the giant would do to us? They'd cut off our privileges.
2ⁿᵈ Guard Yeah! An' 'ave us boiled in noil!
1ˢᵗ Guard Face it, Princess, you're never gonna get out of 'ere.
Primrose (*stepping forward*) Can it be true? Will I never see my home or my dear father again? And what of my darling Tom? Will I ever see him again?

Song 13

Song for Primrose and Children

Slugslime enters from L

Slugslime (*crossing to Primrose, very smarmy*) Ah! Primrose — my dear. Have you come to tell me you have decided to become my bride?
Primrose (*ignoring him and turning to the Guards*) Take me back to my cell and lock me up. I prefer the company of rats to that of this repulsive reptile.

She sweeps out R, *followed by the Guards*

Slugslime (*to audience*) She loves me really. (*Moving to* L, *and addressing the Children*) Pay attention all of you! As you are aware our resident chef has been taken ill. A replacement has been found and she will be in charge. (*Sneering*) Taking her orders from *me*, of course.

Mum enters from R, *followed by Tim and Lucy. All three are wearing aprons and tall chef's hats*

Act II, Scene 5   55

Slugslime Here she is. (*To Mum, indicating the Children*) These are your kitchen staff.
Mum Ooh! Aren't they a bit small?
Tim Perhaps they're — wait for it — *short order* cooks! (*He guffaws*)
Mum Oy! I do the jokes!
Tim Let us know when.
Mum (*to Slugslime*) We can manage on our own. Locally I'm known as the Nigella Lawson of (*local place*)!
Lucy And I'm known as the Delia Smith of (*another local place*).
Tim And I'm known as the Gordon Ramsay of (*yet another local place*)! And if you don't believe it, you can go and ...

Mum clamps her hand over Tim's mouth, and then takes it away

... yourself!

Mum So you see, we don't need any help. You can send the Bash Street Kids (*or something topical*) home.
Slugslime Very well. (*To Children*) Get out!

To suitable music, the Children march out L

Mum Very smart! (*To audience*) I bet they were trained by (*local gag*).
Slugslime (*going to Mum*) Time is running out. You should have one in the oven by now.
Mum I beg your pardon!
Slugslime A cake! My master always has cake for tea. A very large cake! So you'd better get on with it! (*He moves to exit* L) I shall return shortly to see how you are progressing. (*Indicating the audience*) And don't let these pathetic little parasites hold you up!

Snarling at the audience, he exits L

Mum and the others turn and blow a raspberry in his direction

Tim Hey, Mum! What have you done with Tom?
Lucy Yes. Where are you hiding him?

Mum gives a big grin and points to her hat

Tim Oh, I get it! He's gone on — *ahead*! (*He guffaws*)
Mum Hold tight, Tom.

Mum carefully removes her hat and turns it upside down. They all look inside the hat

Mum
Tim } (*together*) Hallo, Tom!
Lucy

Mum He's saying something. What is it, Tom? (*She puts her ear to the hat and listens*) Right ... right... (*To Tim and Lucy*) He says he wants to find out where they're keeping Princess Primrose.
Lucy Don't you think we ought to make him normal size first?
Mum (*to "Tom"*) Do you hear that, Tom? (*Listens at hat*) Yes ... yes ... right. (*To Tim and Lucy*) He says it's better if he stays tiny for the moment. That way he can search about without being seen. (*To "Tom"*) Right, Tom. I'm going to put you down.

Mum goes to the side wing R. *She bends down and places the open end of the hat behind the wing, just out of sight*

Mum Hop out, Tom ... That's it ... Now, you be careful ... Don't get trodden on ... Good luck, my little soldier ... (*She waves to off stage "Tom", and then stands up*) Oh, I hope he'll be all right. (*She puts the hat on*) Let's hope they don't have a cat!
Tim What are we gonna do while he's searching, Mum?
Mum Have a go at makin' Giant Underpants his cake, I suppose. (*To audience*) That'll be a novelty for you, won't it? Watching a bunch of nitwits tryin' to cook against the clock.

They go to the table. Business with mixing bowl, etc.

Mum Now, we'll need some ingredients. I shall want six eggs.
Tim I'll get it!

He dashes out R

Mum And some flour.
Lucy I'll get it!

She dashes out L

Tim returns, carrying a beer keg

Mum What's that?
Tim Six X!

Act II, Scene 5

Mum I said six *eggs*, you wally! Get rid of it! Er ... Put it in my bedroom!
Tim Where do you think I found it?

Tim exits R with keg

Lucy enters L, holding a large bunch of flowers. NOTE: It has a nylon wire attached

Mum What's that?
Lucy Daffodils, tulips and forget-me-nots.
Mum Daffodils, tulips and *what*?
Lucy I forgot.
Mum It's not that sort of flower anyway! I want *baking* flour for cakes.
Lucy You can use these. Look!

The bunch of flowers rises in the air and disappears from sight, accompanied by a suitable sound effect (Swanee whistle or similar)

Lucy Self-raising flower!

Lucy dashes out

Mum (*to audience*) What did I do to deserve this?

Tim enters R, carrying a carton of (rubber) eggs very carefully

Tim Here's the eggs.
Mum Careful! *Careful*!

Tim trips and the eggs fly into the air and bounce around the stage

Mum (*to audience*) It must be a spring chicken!

They retrieve the eggs and put them in the mixing bowl

Lucy enters L with a large flour shaker

Lucy Here's the flour.

Lucy gives the flour to Mum, who shakes it liberally into the bowl and over the others. They all cough and sneeze

Mum We'll want some currants.
Tim Currants! I'll get some!

Tim exits R

Lucy exits L

Tim re-enters holding a tangle of coiled wires

Tim Here's the currents, Mum! (*He tugs at the wire*)

There is a flash. The sound of electrical sparking and crackling is heard. The Lights flicker

Tim receives an electric shock and starts yelling and shaking

Eeeeeee!!

Mum grabs Tom's free hand. The shock is passed on, and she starts yelling and shaking

Lucy enters from L, *with a bag of currants*

Lucy grabs Mum's left hand and also receives the shock. All three are yelling and shaking

There is another flash, a loud bang and a Black-out. NOTE: the wires are removed during the Black-out

Tim, Lucy and Mum collapse in a heap on the floor

The Lights return to normal

Mum (*to audience*) Cor! That was SHOCKING!

Mum, Tim and Lucy stand up

Let that be a lesson to you, kids. Never, never — have a son like him!

They go to the table and dump the bag of currants in the bowl

Lucy What do we need now?

Act II, Scene 5

Mum Some water.
Tim I'll get some!

Tim dashes out R

Mum (*to Lucy*) You'd better get it. He'll probably come back with cement!

Lucy dashes out L

Tim returns, staggering under the weight of a large plastic bucket. NOTE: It is filled with long strips of silver tinsel fixed to the inside of the bucket

Tim Here's the water! (*Staggering down to the front of the stage*) Cor! This is really heavy! It's filled right to the very top! Ooops!

He pretends to trip and throws the contents of the bucket into the audience

Ha! Ha! Ha! That fooled you, didn't it! Ha! Ha! Ha!

Lucy enters from L, *holding a small plastic bucket containing real water*

Still laughing at the audience, Tim blunders into Lucy and she upsets the bucket down his front

Tim Ugh! I'm all wet!
Mum Serves you right, you big drip! Come on, you two! This won't get the cake made!

Tim and Lucy throw their buckets offstage, and then join Mum behind the table

Unseen by the others, Primrose pops her head out from behind the wing on R

Primrose Psst!
Tim (*to Mum*) What?
Mum I didn't say anything.
Tim You psst.
Mum I beg your pardon!
Primrose Psst!

Tim There! You did it again.
Primrose (*emerging into full view*) Over here.
All (*seeing her*) Princess! (*They rush across to join her*)
Lucy Did Tom set you free, Your Highness?
Primrose Yes. He found the key to my cell. Fortunately it's only a small key and he managed to push it under the door so I could let myself out. He told me you were here in the kitchen.
Mum He a right little miracle worker, isn't he? By the way ... er ... what have you done with him?
Primrose Don't worry. I've got him safely tucked away.
Mum (*looking her over*) Er ... dare I ask where? If it's not a rude question.
Primrose (*holding up a drawstring bag*) He's in here!
Mum (*taking the bag and gently feeling it*) Ooh! So he is! (*Tickles the bag*) Itchy-coo!
Primrose Tom told me there's a magic word that will instantly return him to normal size.
Mum Yes. We'd better say it and get out of here before old Slimy comes back!
Slugslime (*off* L, *yelling*) I can't smell anything cooking!

Mum, Primrose, Tim and Lucy fly into a panic

Mum Too late! That's him!
Lucy You'd better hide, Your Highness!
Primrose Where?
Lucy (*lifting up the tablecloth*) Under here! Quick!

Primrose dives out of sight under the table. Mum and the others go behind the table and pretend to be busy at the mixing bowl. In the panic, Mum has put the bag on the table

Slugslime enters from L, *and crosses to the table*

Mum And as I said to Jamie Oliver, you can't beat a nice spotted dick.
Slugslime (*snarling*) Haven't you made that cake yet?
Mum Oh, you can't hurry us professionals. (*She bangs the things around in the bowl*)
Slugslime Are you sure you know what you're doing? That looks a complete mess!
Mum It's our special preparation.
Slugslime (*seeing the bag and picking it up*) And what's this? Is this part of your special preparation too?

Act II, Scene 5

Mum (*yelling in horror*) *That's my son*!!
Slugslime What?
Lucy She means that's her *sun-flower seeds*! They're part of the ingredients.
Slugslime Why haven't you put them in?
Tim They ... they need to be crushed first.
Slugslime Oh, I love crushing things! I'll do it for you.

To the others' horror, Slugslime picks up a large rolling pin and prepares to smash it down on the bag
  Suddenly, the two Guards rush on from R

Guards Master! Master!
Slugslime (*laying down the rolling pin*) What is it?
1st Guard It's the Princess! She's escaped!
Slugslime (*enraged*) *What?!*

  Still clutching the bag, Slugslime rushes out R, *followed by the Guards*

Primrose comes out from under the table

Primrose What's happening?
Lucy Slugslime's found out you've escaped.
Mum And that's not the worse of it! He's just run off with Tom in the bag!
Primrose Oh, no!
Slugslime (*off* R, *yelling*) *You incompetent cretins*!!
Lucy He's coming back! Quick! You'd better hide again!

Primrose dives under the table. Tim starts to crawl after her

Mum (*grabbing his belt and pulling him out*) Not you!

  Still holding the bag, Slugslime storms in from R. *He is followed by the two Guards*

Unseen, Primrose crawls out from under the table and creeps out L

Slugslime (*to the Guards*) She used the key! How did she get hold of the key?

The Guards are nonplussed

You blundering blockheads! She must be here somewhere. She can't get out of the castle. Go and search those corridors thoroughly. I'll search on the other side. Get out!

The Guards rush out R

Slugslime (*to the audience*) Someone must have helped her to escape! And when I get my hands on that someone I will (*in his anger he squeezes and twists the bag*) *squeeze* and *squeeze* and *squeeze* ...
Mum (*letting out a horrified wail*) *No*!!
Slugslime What's the matter with you?
Mum (*trying to appear casual*) It's that bag. It doesn't really go with your outfit, ya know.
Slugslime (*noticing the bag*) Bah!

With a snarl, Slugslime throws the bag into the air. Mum and the others dive to catch it

Slugslime rushes out L

Having retrieved the bag, Mum clutches it lovingly to her bosom

Mum Oh, Tom! My poor little mangled mite!
Lucy Do you think he's all right?
Mum Ooo! I'm frightened to look after all that tough an' rumble! Here goes! (*She gingerly opens the bag and peers inside*) Tom? ... Tom?
Tim Is he in one piece?
Mum (*overjoyed*) Oh, yes! There he is! Shaken but not stirred. Hallo, Tom. (*To audience*) He's all right, folks! What's that, Tom? (*She listens at bag*) Princess Primrose? ... She's under the table ... What? ... No, she's not drunk! She's hiding! Right! (*To others*) He says we've to get the Princess and look for somewhere else to hide. Get 'er nibs out.

Tim and Lucy look under the table

Mum
Lucy } (*together*) *A tiny man?!*
Mum Oh, no! (*To "Tom"*) You hear that, Tom? She's gone! What are we gonna do now? (*She listens*) Yes ... Right ...

The Guards enter from R *as Mum is listening and talking. This is unseen by the others*

Act II, Scene 5

Mum Yes ... What was that, Tom? Speak a bit slower, Tom ... Yes ... yes ...
1st Guard Oy!

Mum and the others react. Mum quickly shuts the bag. At this point positions should be: Guards R, Mum RC, Lucy C and Tim LC

Mum, Lucy and Tim try to adopt a nonchalant air

1st Guard Who were you talkin' to? Who's in that bag?
Mum In *this* bag? You must be having illuminations. How could there be anyone in this little tiny bag? (*To others*) Oh, he's a Silly Billy, isn't he?
All three give forced laughs

1st Guard Let's 'ave a look! (*He reaches for the bag*)
Mum No!

Slugslime enters L

Mum passes the bag to Lucy, who passes it on to Tim. He passes it on to Slugslime!

Slugslime (*snarling*) Why have I got this wretched bag again?
1st Guard There's someone in it, master. The old biddy was talkin' to 'im!
2nd Guard Yeah! She called 'im Tom.
Slugslime *Tom*! I wonder ... (*to Guards*) Seize them!

The Guards grab Mum and the others. Slugslime undoes the bag and looks inside. He gives his evil laugh. Primrose peeps out from behind the L wing

Slugslime Tom Thumb! So! You have managed to make yourself small again, I see! No doubt you are responsible for setting the princess free! Ha! Ha! Ha! Well, you won't get a second chance! I'm going to squash you like a bug! (*He puts his hand inside the bag. He lets out a yell of agony and drops the bag to the floor*) Agggh! (*Holding up a finger*) HE BIT ME!!

Primrose dashes forward, picks up the bag, and runs off with it L

Snarling with rage, Slugslime rushes out after her

Tim (*pointing upwards*) *LOOK!!*

The Guards look up

Tim pushes Mum and Lucy off R, *and exits after them*

When the Guards realize they've been tricked, they run off in pursuit

NOTE: If desired, suitable "chase" music can be played to accompany the following sequence

Primrose runs on from UL, *being pursued by Slugslime, and out* UR. *Mum, Tim and Lucy, being chased by the Guards, run on from* DR, *and out* DL. *Primrose, pursued by Slugslime, runs on from* UR, *and out* UL. *The Guards run on from* DL, *being chased by Mum, Tim and Lucy. Halfway across the stage they realize their mistake and stop. They all about-turn and the Guards chase Mum and the others off* DL. *Primrose runs on from* UR, *and out* UL. *Slugslime runs on from* UR. *Mum, Tim and Lucy run on from* DL. *They see Slugslime and let out a yell. They turn tail and run out* DL. *They immediately reappear, being chased by the Guards, and out* DR

Slugslime goes up and hides behind the table

Primrose runs on from UL. *Thinking she is alone, she pauses to check that Tom is safe in the bag*

Slugslime emerges and creeps up behind Primrose. He goes to make a grab for her

Primrose hears something and runs off DR

Slugslime snarls and hides behind the table again

Mum, Tim and Lucy creep on backwards from R. *At the same time, the Guards creep on backwards from* L. *Eventually their posteriors touch and they turn to see each other. They all let out a yell and run out the same way they came in*

Slugslime rises from behind the table and snarls at the audience

Primrose runs on from L. *Slugslime disappears from sight again*

Act II, Scene 5

Mum, Lucy and Tim creep on backwards from DR. *Primrose taps Mum on the shoulder, making her jump with fright. Primrose indicates the exit* UL, *and they move towards it*

The Guards suddenly appear at exit UL. *Mum, Lucy, Primrose and Tim pull up short*

Slugslime emerges from behind the table and sneaks down to beside Tim. Primrose passes the bag to Mum, who passes it on to Lucy, who passes it on to Tim, who passes it on to Slugslime!

Slugslime (*holding the bag and laughing triumphantly*) Ha! Ha! Ha!

If used, the chase music stops

Tim snatches the bag from Slugslime and runs off R *with it*

Slugslime dashes off in pursuit

The Guards grab Primrose and the others and herd them to UL

Slugslime returns holding Tim in one hand and the bag in the other. NOTE: This is now a duplicate bag with a nylon line attached. (See Production Notes.) Slugslime pushes Tim across to join the others

Slugslime (*moving to* LC) Ha! Ha! Ha! And now, Tom Thumb, I am going to finish you off once and for all! Ha! Ha! Ha! (*He puts the bag on the ground*) It is time I put my foot down — hard! (*With evil relish, he raises his foot and goes to stamp on bag*)

But the bag slides out of the way just in time! It should appear that tiny Tom is propelling the bag himself from the inside. Again Slugslime stamps, and again the bag slides away. This business is repeated, with Slugslime getting more and more infuriated

Primrose (*to Mum*) The magic word! *Say the magic word!*
Mum Er. Oh, no! I've forgotten it!
Tim (*to audience*) What is it, folks?
Audience *ALAKAZAM*!!

There is a flash, followed by a complete Black-out. Music plays and magical sounds fill the air. NOTE: The bag is removed during the Black-out

Tom enters

The Lights return to normal. The full-sized Tom is standing there. The music and sounds fade out. Slugslime reacts and staggers back

The Guards yell with fright and run out L

Slugslime sneaks out DR

Tom and Primrose rush into each other's arms

Primrose Tom!
Tom Primrose!
Tom (*to others*) Thanks for saving me from being flattened.
Mum Don't thank us. We forgot the magic word. Thank our friends out there.
Tom (*to audience*) Thanks, everyone.
Tim (*looking around*) Hey! Where's Slugslime?
Mum I don't know and I don't care.
Tom Let's get out of here while there's no one about.

A splintering sound followed by a loud crash is heard off stage R. *All react*

Lucy (*clinging to Tim*) Ooh! It's the giant!

The King, wearing a suit of dented armour, and carrying a bent sword, clanks on from R. *He raises his visor to reveal himself*

King Never fear, your king is here!

The Citizens enter from R *with Spellena who is wearing a hooded cloak to conceal her identity. She remains in the background*

Primrose (*rushing to him*) Father! How did you get in?
King I decided it was high time I acted like a *real* king, m'dear. We smashed down the castle doors and I'm here to rescue you! (*Full of bravado*) Where's that villain Slugslime? After I've dealt with him I'm going to sort out that pesky giant as well! (*Brandishing his sword*) Have at you!
Primrose Let's just settle for getting out of here, shall we?
King What? Oh! Right you are, m'dear. (*Pointing with sword to* R) This way!

Act II, Scene 5

Slugslime springs on from L

Slugslime Not so fast! You don't think you're going to get out of here alive, do you? The giant is on his way here now! He will squash you all like ants! Ha! Ha! Ha! Here he comes!

The sounds of slow, heavy footsteps are heard approaching from off R. *As before, they reverberate around the stage and auditorium*

The lighting becomes dark and sinister

Tom, Primrose, Tim, Lucy, King and Mum back away and cling to each other in terrified groups

The footsteps come to a halt. The Giant's booming laughter and voice is heard

Giant (*off, bellowing*) HO! HO! HO! HO!
        You have dared to enter my private domain.
        For that you will suffer the ultimate pain!
        I will squash you all like a troublesome fly!
        I am coming to get you! So *prepare to die*!

The others wail and scream in terror

Spellena moves quickly to the front. She throws back her hood to reveal herself

Tom Spellena!
King You didn't think I'd come without reinforcements, did you?
Spellena (*facing* R, *and addressing the off stage giant*)
        Get back, you monstrous bag of wind!
        For far too long you have erred and sinned.
        No longer will you terrorise,
        For *you* I mean to — *miniaturize*!

Spellena makes magic pass to off R

There is a blinding flash from off R

The Giant roars. This gradually diminishes into a childish squeak

The lighting returns to previous setting

A very irate miniature Giant scampers on from R. *NOTE: This is a small child costumed as in the Giant's portrait with huge beard, etc.*

The others, including Slugslime, can't believe their eyes

Little Giant (*to Spellena, in an angry squeak*) What have you done to me?! What have you done to me?!

Squealing with rage, the little Giant scampers out L

Slugslime Master!
Spellena (*to Slugslime*) And now to deal with you!
          You used your magic with evil in mind.
          You don't deserve to be one of our kind.
          I will remedy that without further delay,
             By taking your magical powers — away! (*She makes a magic pass at Slugslime*)

There is a flash

Slugslime makes magic passes at the others. Nothing happens. He repeats the process on the audience, and still nothing happens

Mum Ha! Ha! His Duracell's run out!
Slugslime Oh, no! All my lovely magic powers have gone! (*A broken man*) I'm nothing without them! No one will want to know me now.

The Crone enters beside him

Crone Oh, I wouldn't say that. (*She slips her arm through his*) I quite fancy you really! (*She gives him a toothless grin*)
Slugslime (*groaning*) Oh, no!
Crone (*to audience*) Well, beggars can't be choosers, can they, girls? (*To Slugslime*) Come on. You're taking me to (*local club*) tonight. And who knows, you might get lucky.

The Crone pulls Slugslime towards the exit, L. *He still manages to give the others, and the audience, a snarl as he is hauled out*

The others laugh

Tom We can't thank you enough, Spellena. You saved our lives.
Primrose And rid us of the giant and that evil Slugslime.

Act II, Scene 6   69

Spellena It was my pleasure.
King I say! This calls for a celebration of some kind.
Tom You're right, Your Majesty. And I know just the thing. Because of the giant we've all been starving for weeks, haven't we?
All Yes!
Tom Well, this castle is full of food.
All Our food!
Tom Right! So why don't we have a giant-size banquet?
All Hurrah!

Song 14

Led by Tom and Primrose, they all perform a joyful song and dance. The number ends with a tableau

Tabs close or the "Lane" front cloth is lowered

Scene 6

Before the banquet

Tabs, or the front cloth used in Act I, Scene 2

The little Giant scampers on from DL

Little Giant (*to audience*) Does anyone know where I can get a Gro-bag?

He scampers out DR

Arm-in-arm, the Crone and a very miserable-looking Slugslime enter DL. *She leads him reluctantly across the stage and out* DR

Tim and Lucy enter DL

Tim }
Lucy } (*waving to the audience, together*) Hallo, folks! Hi, kids!
Tim Well, that's it. It's nearly all over. Aaaaahh!

Tim and Lucy encourage the audience to sigh with them

Lucy Have you enjoyed yourselves?
Audience (*we hope!*) Yes!

Tim Why, what have you been doing? (*He guffaws*) Everything has turned out great, hasn't it? We've cut that nasty giant down to size and got rid of old Mr Slimy.
Lucy And Tom and Princess Primrose are going to be married. But the best news is — Timmy and I have just got engaged.

They act all soppy

Tim You liked seeing my giant marrow, didn't you, Lucy?
Lucy Oh, yes!
Tim Well, now that we're engaged I've got something else to show you.
Lucy (*thrilled*) Ooo! Timmy!
Tim It's my giant pumpkin!

Lucy is disappointed, but still manages to give him a cuddle

Mum enters from DR

Mum Oh, no! I see (*current romantic couple on TV*) are at it again! (*Going to them*) Oy! Put each other down for a minute. I need your help. Y'know we're going to the big banquet at the royal palace tonight?
Tim
Lucy } (*together*) Yes.
Mum Well, the king has asked me to handle his arrangements.
Tim Cor!
Mum No, you twit! He wants me to sort out the music. Find some songs to sing. Have you got any ideas?
Tim I know! How about — (*He does his loud, off-key rendering as before*)

Mum and Lucy shut Tim up

Lucy I know a brilliant song.
Tim What's that, Lucy?

Lucy names the chosen song

Mum Oh, yes! That's a good one! Everybody can sing that.
Tim (*indicating the audience*) Even our mates out there?
Mum Well, let's try 'em out, shall we? (*To audience*) You knew that was coming, didn't you? There's no gettin' out of it! We've locked all the doors. (*To Tim*) They'll need the words.

Act II, Scene 7

Tim I've got the sheets.
Mum They don't need to know *that*!
Tim The *song sheets* with the words on!

Tim and Lucy exit and return with the song sheets

They hold them up. Tim's sheet is showing the blank side

Mum (*pointing to his sheet*) What's this? There's nothin' on it!
Tim I know. It's — *Silent Night*! (*He guffaws and turns the sheet the right way*)
Mum (*to audience*) He can't help it. His father spent a lot of time in (*local place*)! Right then, my little song birds. It's time to see what you can do. We'll start it off, then you can all join in. (*To Conductor/ Pianist*) Ready when you are, Elton.

Song 15

They have fun getting the audience to participate. The house lights come up as children are invited on stage to sing. After singing, they are asked their names and ages, etc. Tim and Lucy give them sweets, and they return to their seats. The house lights go down

Waving goodbye to the audience, Mum, Tim and Lucy run out

The Lights fade to Black-out

A fanfare sounds

The Lights come up on —

Scene 7

The Grand Finale

A special Finale setting or the Royal Gardens set can be used with added fairy lights

Bright lighting and bouncy music

The full company enter to take their bows. The last to enter are Tom and Primrose, magnificently attired

Tom	I'm back to normal, as large as life.
Primrose	And very soon I shall be his wife.
King	I'm proud to have Tom for a son-in law.
Mum	That makes me royalty! (*Posh laugh*) Haw! Haw! Haw!
Lucy	Timmy's buying me a ring tomorrow.
Tim	That means I'll have to flog my marrow!
Slugslime	I'd get my revenge if I still had my magic.
Crone	You've got me now, so don't look so tragic.
Little Giant	I'm a giant no more and I've lost my home.
Mum	You can hire yourself out as a garden gnome.
Spellena	We hope you have enjoyed your stay.
Tim	And your bums are not too numb.
Spellena	There is only one thing left to say —
All (*waving*)	Goodbye — from young Tom Thumb!

Song 16 (or a reprise)

CURTAIN

FURNITURE AND PROPERTY LIST

Further dressing may be added at the director's discretion

ACT I

Scene 1

On stage: Palace side entrance and steps
Backcloth and groundrow showing palace gardens
Wings representing trees, bushes and flower beds

Off stage: Trolley. *On it*: "Heath Robinson"-style tea urn (*in it*: smoke effect/apparatus for exploding tea urn sequence), cups, boxes with small packets of biscuits, large mallet. (**Mum Thumb**)
Tridents (**Demons**)

Personal: **King**: gardening magazine

Scene 2

On stage: Tabs, or lane frontcloth showing giant's castle in the distance

Off stage: Large basket of bread (**1st Citizen**)
Large truckle of cheese (**2nd Citizen**)
Pile of cans (**3rd Citizen**)
Tall cake (**4th Citizen**)
Long string of large (prop) sausages (**Children**)

Personal: **Mum Thumb**: large wedge of (prop) cheese

Scene 3

On stage: Cottage interior backcloth
Cottage interior wings
Table. *On it*: Cloth reaching to ground, dressing, "trick" basket. *Under it*: Puppeteer with "thumb size" Tom finger puppet

Off stage: Tridents (**Demons**)

Scene 4

On stage: Tabs, or lane front cloth used in Act I, Scene 2

Off stage: Basket and "thumb size" Tom finger puppet (**Mum Thumb**)

Scene 5

On stage: Throne room back wall with arched window in centre
Throne room wings
Throne
Backcloth or cyclorama behind back wall

Off stage: Basket and finger puppet (**Mum Thumb**)
Giant eye (**SM**)
Giant hand (**SM**)

Personal: **King**: bag of jelly babies

ACT II

Scene 1

On stage: Weird Wood wings
Weird Wood backcloth and ground row
Front of small thatched cottage with practical door

Off stage: Basket and finger puppet (**Mum Thumb**)

Personal: **Spellena**: Small packet

Scene 2

On stage: Tabs, or lane front cloth used in Act I, Scene 2

Scene 3

On stage: Royal Gardens set used in Act I, Scene 1

Off stage: Basket (**Tim**)

Personal: **King**: Handkerchief

Scene 4

On stage: Tabs, or lane front cloth used in Act I, Scene 2

Furniture and Property List

Off stage: Basket and finger puppet (**Mum Thumb**)

SCENE 5

On stage: Kitchen backcloth
Kitchen wings
Table. *On it*: Cloth that reaches the ground, large mixing bowl, wooden spoon, rolling pin, cooking paraphernalia

Off stage: Beer keg (**Tim**)
Bunch of flowers with nylon line attached (**Lucy** and **SM**)
Carton of (rubber) eggs (**Tim**)
Flour shaker (**Lucy**)
Length of coiled wires (**Tim**)
Bag of currants (**Lucy**)
Large plastic bucket. *In it*: long strips of tinsel fixed to the inside (**Tim**)
Small plastic bucket. *In it*: water (**Lucy**)
Drawstring bag (**Primrose**)
Duplicate drawstring bag with nylon line attached (**Slugslime** and **SM**)

Personal: **King**: bent sword

SCENE 6

On stage: Tabs, or lane front cloth

Off stage: Song sheets (**Tim** and **Lucy**)

SCENE 7

On stage: Special Finale setting, or Royal Gardens set used in Act I, Scene 1 with added decorations and fairy lights

LIGHTING PLOT

Property fittings: nil
Various interior and exterior settings

ACT I

Scene 1

To open:	General exterior lighting	
Cue 1	Song 2 *Romantic lighting and follow spots on* **Primrose** *and* **Tom**	(Page 4)
Cue 2	End of Song 2 *Take out spots and romantic lighting. Return to previous setting*	(Page 4)
Cue 3	**Mum:** "...left their teeth at home." *Bring up house lights*	(Page 9)
Cue 4	**Tim** and **Lucy** return to stage *Fade out house lights*	(Page 10)
Cue 5	**King**: "I repeat — he will not be coming here!" *Flash of lightning. Dark and sinister lighting*	(Page 12)
Cue 6	Song 4 (Demon dance) *Special lighting*	(Page 12)
Cue 7	End of Song 4 *Take out special lighting. Return to dark and eerie lighting*	(Page 12)
Cue 8	**Slugslime** appears from DL *Lighting becomes brighter, but still remains eerie and sinister*	(Page 12)
Cue 9	**Slugslime**: "*THE GIANT!*" *Flash of lightning*	(Page 13)
Cue 10	Reprise of Song 4 *Special lighting*	(Page 16)
Cue 11	End of Song 4 *Take out special lighting. Lights fade to black-out*	(Page 16)

Lighting Plot

Scene 2

To open:	General exterior lighting	
Cue 12	Song 5 *Follow spots on* **Tim** *and* **Lucy**	(Page 17)
Cue 13	End of Song 5 *Take out follow spots*	(Page 17)
Cue 14	**Slugslime** runs out DR *Fade to black-out*	(Page 20)

Scene 3

To open:	General interior lighting	
Cue 15	**Slugslime**: "... *my magical powers!* Ha! Ha! Ha!" *Lighting becomes strange and eerie*	(Page 24)
Cue 16	**Slugslime**: "*ATMAZOOM!!*". There is a flash *Complete black-out*	(Page 25)
Cue 17	**Tom** exits *Return to previous eerie lighting. Spotlight on basket*	(Page 25)
Cue 18	**Demons** exit *Take out eerie lighting and return to general interior setting. Spotlight remains on basket*	(Page 26)
Cue 19	**Mum**: " ... Gently does it!" *Take out spot. Lights fade to black-out*	(Page 28)

Scene 4

To open:	General exterior lighting	
Cue 20	**Mum**: "Handbrake off, dear!" *House lights up*	(Page 30)
Cue 21	End of Song 7 *House lights down*	(Page 30)
Cue 22	**Lucy** drags **Tim** out *Fade to black-out*	(Page 31)

Scene 5

To open:	General interior lighting	
Cue 23	Song 8 *Follow spot on* **Primrose**	(Page 33)
Cue 24	End of Song 8 *Take out follow spot*	(Page 33)
Cue 25	Giant's footsteps are heard approaching *Lighting takes on an unearthly glow*	(Page 37)
Cue 26	Giant eye appears at window *Eerie spotlight on eye*	(Page 37)
Cue 27	Giant eye disappears from window *Take out eerie spotlight. Return to general interior lighting*	(Page 38)

ACT II

Scene 1

To open:	General exterior lighting. Dappled sunlight effect	
Cue 28	**Spellena**: "That's it. Now I'm ready!" *Lighting becomes magical*	(Page 43)
Cue 29	**Spellena** makes magic pass at "Tom". There is a flash *Complete black-out*	(Page 43)
Cue 30	**Tom** enters and jumps into **Mum's** arms *Return to previous dappled sunlight setting*	(Page 43)
Cue 31	**Tom** and the others exit *Fade to black-out*	(Page 44)

Scene 2

To open: General exterior lighting

Cue 32	Song 10a *Fade out general lighting. Spotlight on Tom*	(Page 46)
Cue 33	End of Song 10a *Fade out spotlight to black-out*	(Page 47)

Lighting Plot

Scene 3

To open:	General exterior lighting	
Cue 34	**Slugslime**: "Ha! Ha! Ha!" *Flashes of lightning. Lighting becomes dark and eerie*	(Page 48)
Cue 35	**Slugslime**: "*CUT!!*" *Lightning flashes stop abruptly. Quick return to previous exterior lighting*	(Page 48)
Cue 36	**Spellena**: "And now to make you tiny Tom once more" *Lighting becomes magical*	(Page 50)
Cue 37	**Spellena** makes magic pass at **Tom**. There is a flash *Complete black-out*	(Page 50)

Scene 4

To open:	General exterior lighting	
Cue 38	Song 12 *Follow spot on* **Crone**	(Page 50)
Cue 39	End of Song 12 *Take out spot*	(Page 51)
Cue 40	Lucy drags Tim out DL *Fade to black-out*	(Page 53)

Scene 5

To open:	General interior lighting	
Cue 41	Song 13 *Romantic lighting. Follow spot on* **Primrose** *and* **Children**	(Page 54)
Cue 42	End of Song 13 *Take out spot and return to general interior lighting*	(Page 54)
Cue 43	**Tim** tugs at the wire. There is a flash *General lighting flickers*	(Page 58)
Cue 44	**Mum**, **Tim** and **Lucy** are yelling and shaking. There is a flash *Complete black-out*	(Page 58)

Cue 45	**Tim**, **Lucy** and **Mum** collapse in a heap on the floor *Return to general interior lighting*	(Page 58)
Cue 46	**Audience**: "*ALAKAZAM!!*". There is a flash *Complete black-out*	(Page 65)
Cue 47	**Tom** enters *Lighting returns to previous, general interior setting*	(Page 66)
Cue 48	**Giant's** footsteps are heard approaching *Lighting becomes dark and sinister*	(Page 67)
Cue 49	The **Giant's** roaring gradually diminishes *Lighting returns to previous, general interior setting*	(Page 67)
Cue 50	**Little Giant** enters *Follow spot*	(Page 68)
Cue 51	**Little Giant** exits *Take out spot*	(Page 68)

SCENE 6

To open:	General exterior lighting	
Cue 52	Song 15 *Bring up house lights*	(Page 71)
Cue 53	Children from audience return to their seats *Take out house lights*	(Page 71)
Cue 54	**Mum**, **Tim** and **Lucy** run out *Fade to black-out*	(Page 71)

SCENE 7

To open: Bright general lighting with follow spots on Cast as they enter and take their bows

No cues

EFFECTS PLOT
ACT I

Cue 1	**1st Citizen:** "Here he comes!" *A fanfare sounds*	(Page 2)
Cue 2	**Mum** hits urn with mallet *The urn starts to vibrate and make strange, gurgling noises*	(Page 10)
Cue 3	**Mum, Tim** and **Lucy** back away nervously to the other side of the stage *The urn's vibrations and noises increase*	(Page 11)
Cue 4	**Lucy**: "Oh, Timmy! What's it doing?" *The urn rocks about, and the sound changes to a loud, high pitched whine*	(Page 11)
Cue 5	**Mum**: "*She's gonna BLOW!!!*" *Blinding flash and loud bang as the urn explodes. The lid flies off and smoke billows out*	(Page 11)
Cue 6	There's a flash of lightning *Loud clap of thunder*	(Page 12)
Cue 7	**Demons** face L, kneel and bow their heads *Flash and puff of smoke*	(Page 12)
Cue 8	There's a flash of lightning *Clap of thunder*	(Page 13)
Cue 9	**Slugslime**: "Ha! Ha! Ha!" *Weird sounds fill the air*	(Page 24)
Cue 10	**Slugslime**: "*ATMAZOOM!!*" *Flash. Weird sounds become louder*	(Page 25)
Cue 11	**Tom** exits *The weird sounds decrease in volume*	(Page 25)
Cue 12	**Slugslime** and **Demons** exit *Fade out weird sounds*	(Page 26)

Cue 13	**Slugslime**: "Here he comes now!"	(Page 36)
	Sound of Giant's huge, heavy footsteps approaching	
Cue 14	**Slugslime** is revelling in fiendish glee	(Page 37)
	Footsteps come to a halt	
Cue 15	**Giant**: "HO! HO! HO!"	(Page 37)
	Giant eye appears at window	
Cue 16	**Primrose**: "Father...!"	(Page 37)
	Giant hand slides on	
Cue 17	**Giant**: "HO! HO! HO!"	(Page 38)
	Giant hand slides off holding Primrose	
Cue 18	**King**: "Primrose! Primrose!"	(Page 38)
	Giant eye disappears from window	

ACT II

Cue 19	**Spellena** makes magic pass at **Tom**	(Page 43)
	There's a flash. Magical sounds fill the air	
Cue 20	**Tom** enters and jumps into **Mum's** arms. Lighting returns to normal	(Page 43)
	Magical sounds fade out	
Cue 21	**Slugslime**: "...work in sorcery! Ha! Ha! Ha!"	(Page 48)
	Claps of thunder. Sinister music plays	
Cue 22	**Slugslime**: "*CUT!!*"	(Page 48)
	Claps of thunder stop abruptly	
Cue 23	**Spellena**: "...tiny Tom Thumb once more"	(Page 50)
	Magical sounds fill the air	
Cue 24	**Spellena** makes magic pass at Tom	(Page 50)
	Flash. Magical sounds become louder and continue during the scene change. Fade out sounds as lights come up on next scene	
Cue 25	**Lucy**: "You can use these. Look!"	(Page 57)
	Sound effect (Swanee whistle) as bunch of flowers rises into the air (on nylon line) and disappears into the flies	

Effects Plot 83

Cue 27	**Tim** tugs at wire Flash. *Sound of electrical sparking and crackling*	(Page 58)
Cue 28	**Mum**, **Tim**, and **Lucy** are all yelling and shaking *Flash, followed by black-out. Sounds stop abruptly*	(Page 58)
Cue 29	For chase sequence (optional). **Primrose** runs on from UL *Pre-recorded "fast" music*	(Page 64)
Cue 30	End of chase sequence (optional). **Slugslime** holds up the bag and gives a triumphant laugh *Cut "fast" music*	(Page 65)
Cue 31	**Slugslime** goes to stamp on bag *The bag moves away (on nylon line). This is repeated several times*	(Page 65)
Cue 32	Audience: "*ALAKAZAM!!*" *Flash. Magical sounds fill the air*	(Page 65)
Cue 33	**Tom** enters and lighting returns to previous setting *Fade out magical sounds*	(Page 66)
Cue 34	**Tom**: "...while there's no one about" *Sound of splintering, followed by a loud crash off* R	(Page 66)
Cue 35	**Slugslime**: "Ha! Ha! Ha! Here he comes!" *Sound of Giant's huge, heavy footsteps approaching off* R. *They reverberate around the stage and auditorium*	(Page 67)
Cue 36	**Tom**, **Primrose**, **Tim**, **Lucy**, **King** and **Mum** back away and cling to each other in terrified groups *Giant's footsteps come to a halt*	(Page 67)
Cue 37	**Spellena** makes magic pass to off R *Blinding flash off* R	(Page 67)
Cue 38	**Spellena** makes magic pass at **Slugslime** *Flash*	(Page 68)
Cue 39	End of Scene 6 (Lights fade to Black-out) *Fanfare sounds*	(Page 71)

www.ingramcontent.com/pod-product-compliance
Lightning Source LLC
LaVergne TN
LVHW051751080426
835511LV00018B/3298